LIMITLESS
THINKING

LIMITLESS THINKING

CHANGE YOUR MIND, CHANGE YOUR WORLD

DARRIN ELFORD

ISBN: 978-1-991363-31-2 (Paperback)

eISBN: 978-1-991363-32-9 (E-Book)

First edition

Acknowledgements

I would like to express my deepest gratitude to all those who have supported me throughout the journey of creating this book. To my family and friends, whose unwavering belief in me fuelled my determination to bring this vision to life—thank you for your encouragement, love, and endless patience.

I also want to acknowledge the countless individuals whose stories of resilience, courage, and transformation inspired me every step of the way. Your experiences remind me that we all have the power to break through our limitations and live a life filled with purpose and possibility.

Finally, to the readers—thank you for embracing this journey of limitless thinking. Your commitment to personal growth is a testament to the amazing potential within all of us. May you continue to live boldly and fearlessly as you create your own limitless reality.

Table of Contents

Introduction – The Power of Limitless Thinking

Understanding the Power of Limitless Thinking

Limitless thinking is not just about dreaming big or believing in fantasies. It's about understanding that your mind has the extraordinary ability to break through any barriers you've placed around yourself. At its core, limitless thinking is the belief that there are no real limits to what you can achieve—no matter where you've been, what you've faced, or how many times you've fallen short in the past.

For most of us, life can feel like we're constantly up against walls. We hear the voices of doubt, fear, and insecurity telling us that we're not good enough, that our dreams are too big, or that we're destined to fail. Limitless thinking is about rejecting these constraints. It's a mindset shift, a conscious decision to believe that your potential isn't determined by your past, your circumstances, or your self-imposed limitations.

It's the realization that you don't have to stay stuck in patterns of negativity or self-doubt. You can choose to see the world through a different lens—one that focuses on possibilities instead of problems. You can train your mind to see opportunity in challenges, strength in adversity, and success in what once seemed impossible. When you think limitlessly, you open yourself to a future of growth, transformation, and endless potential.

Think about it: Every major breakthrough in human history—from technology to art to science—was once considered impossible. And yet, someone somewhere decided to believe that what the world thought was impossible could be made possible. That's the essence of limitless thinking. It's about knowing that if someone else can break through, so can you.

You may be wondering, "How do I begin to think limitlessly?" It starts with the simple, powerful idea that you're not limited by anything other than your own thoughts. The more you begin to challenge your negative beliefs, the more you'll

11

see just how much room you have to grow. This book will guide you through that process and help you tap into the incredible power of your mind, allowing you to change your world in ways you never thought possible.

Limitless thinking isn't just a theory—it's a lifestyle, a way of being that transforms the way you approach life, challenges, and success. When you embrace it, the world around you shifts. Opportunities appear, confidence builds, and you start to feel like the person you've always known you could be.

Breaking Free from Mental Barriers

We all have mental barriers—those invisible walls we've built in our minds that limit our potential. They are the doubts, fears, and beliefs that tell us we can't, we're not enough, or it's too late. These barriers hold us back from taking risks, pursuing our dreams, and stepping into the life we truly want. The problem is, most of these barriers are not real. They're simply stories we've been telling ourselves for so long that we've started to believe they're facts.

The first step to breaking free from these mental barriers is to acknowledge that they exist. You can't fight what you don't see. Maybe you've told yourself that you'll never succeed because you failed in the past, or maybe you believe you're not smart enough, talented enough, or worthy enough to reach your goals. These thoughts create a prison in your mind—a prison that keeps you stuck, even when the door is wide open.

But here's the truth: the only thing keeping you locked in that prison is your own mind. Your fears, insecurities, and limiting beliefs are the bars that hold you in place. The good news is, you have the key. That key is awareness—the realization that these mental barriers are not permanent truths, but rather, temporary obstacles that can be overcome with effort and intention.

So how do you break free?

It starts with challenging your beliefs. Every time a limiting thought pops into your head, ask yourself, "Is this really true?" Often, the answer will be no. "I'm not good enough" is not a fact—it's a feeling, a thought, and one that can be changed. Instead of accepting it, replace it with a new, empowering belief: "I am enough, just as I am."

Next, begin to question the stories you've been telling yourself. These stories might have served you once, but they no longer hold the power they once did. The story that says you're not capable or that you'll never succeed is just a narrative. And you have the power to rewrite it. Start small by focusing on one belief you'd like to change. Then, take baby steps every day to prove to yourself that it's not true. The more you challenge your mental barriers, the easier it becomes to see past them.

Another powerful tool is visualization. Picture yourself living the life you desire. See yourself succeeding, taking risks, and stepping confidently into new opportunities. When you visualize success, you're rewiring your brain to believe that it's not only possible but inevitable. Your mind doesn't know the difference between a real experience and one vividly imagined. The more you visualize breaking through your mental barriers, the more real that future becomes.

Finally, take action. Even if it's just a small step, taking action proves to your brain that you're not bound by those mental walls. Action is the antidote to fear. Every time you take a step forward, no matter how small, you weaken the hold that fear and doubt have over you.

Breaking free from mental barriers doesn't happen overnight—it's a process. But the more you challenge your old beliefs and replace them with new, empowering ones, the easier it becomes to move beyond your limits. And the more you do it, the more you'll see that the walls you once thought were insurmountable were never as strong as they seemed.

You are not confined by your past or your thoughts. You are capable of so much more than you realize. The first step is to believe that you can break free—and then, take the actions that will set you free.

How Our Thoughts Shape Our Reality

Have you ever noticed how your thoughts can change the way you feel, even the way you see the world? One moment you might be thinking about a difficult situation, and suddenly, everything seems overwhelming. The world feels heavy, and your energy drains. Then, you shift your thoughts—maybe you remember something positive or think about a solution—and suddenly, the weight lifts, and possibilities appear. It's like a light turning on in a dark room.

This is because our thoughts are incredibly powerful. In fact, they don't just influence how we feel in the moment; they actively shape the reality we experience. What we think about ourselves, our circumstances, and the world around us directly impacts how we interact with life. The truth is, we create our reality with the thoughts we choose to entertain.

Think of your mind as a filter. Every moment, your brain is constantly processing thousands of thoughts. Some of those thoughts are positive, while others are negative. But it's the ones we focus on that begin to shape the way we experience our lives. If you constantly think about your limitations, failures, and fears, your mind will begin to look for evidence of those things. You'll see more of what you're focusing on—more failure, more reasons to be afraid, and more obstacles in your path.

On the other hand, when you begin to focus on possibilities, opportunities, and the belief that you are capable of overcoming challenges, your mind starts to look for evidence of those things. You begin to see opportunities where others see problems. You feel empowered to take risks and try new things. You start to feel like the world is working with you instead of against you.

The reality is, the thoughts you choose to believe are not just random—they directly influence the way you act and the results you get. When you tell yourself, "I'm not good enough," you might avoid trying new things or give up before you even start. But when you tell yourself, "I can do this. I am capable of learning and growing," you'll take more action, seek out solutions, and push through obstacles. Your thoughts dictate your behavior, and your behavior determines your results.

There's a concept called the "self-fulfilling prophecy," which is when you believe something to be true, and that belief shapes your actions and outcomes. For example, if you believe that you are destined to fail, you may not give your best effort, and that lack of effort could lead to failure. But if you believe success is possible, you'll be more motivated, persistent, and resourceful in your actions. Your thoughts set the tone for your experiences.

Here's the key takeaway: your thoughts are not just abstract ideas—they are the blueprint for your life. The thoughts you entertain today are building the life you'll live tomorrow. If you want to change your reality, you need to start by changing your thinking.

This is not about ignoring life's difficulties or pretending that everything is perfect. It's about consciously choosing to focus on thoughts that empower you and support the life you want to create. It's about shifting from a mindset of scarcity to one of abundance, from doubt to possibility, and from fear to courage.

So, the next time you catch yourself thinking, "This is too hard" or "I'll never succeed," pause and ask yourself: "What if this could be easier? What if I am more capable than I think?" Replacing negative, limiting thoughts with empowering ones is the first step toward creating a new reality. And remember, your mind doesn't know the difference between what's real and what's imagined. So, if you begin to believe in the possibility of success, your brain will start working with you to make it happen.

The truth is, your thoughts hold the key to the life you want to live. They are the starting point for every change, every breakthrough, and every possibility you'll ever experience. Change your thoughts, and you can change your entire world.

The Journey Ahead: From Despair to Abundance

At this very moment, you may feel overwhelmed, stuck, or even hopeless. Perhaps you're facing challenges that seem insurmountable, or you're living with a constant sense of dissatisfaction that leaves you questioning whether things will ever get better. The weight of despair can feel heavy, and the belief that life could be different may seem far out of reach. But I want to tell you something that may feel hard to believe right now: **Abundance is waiting for you.** Not just material abundance, but an abundance of peace, joy, opportunity, and strength.

The journey ahead is one of transformation—a shift in mindset that will take you from a place of feeling lost and defeated to one where you embrace the endless possibilities that life offers. It's a journey that begins in the darkness of despair but moves toward the light of abundance. And the truth is, **this transformation begins with one simple choice: you can choose to believe that change is possible.**

When you're trapped in despair, everything feels heavy. You see challenges everywhere, and the thought of making a change can feel exhausting. It's as though you're stuck in a cycle that you can't escape from. But this cycle isn't your fate—it's simply the result of a mindset that has been shaped by fear, doubt, and limiting beliefs.

Moving from despair to abundance doesn't mean that all of a sudden, your problems will vanish. Life will still present challenges, and there will be difficult moments. But the key is that your mindset will shift from seeing obstacles as roadblocks to seeing them as stepping stones to something greater. In a mindset of abundance, challenges become opportunities for growth, and setbacks become lessons that strengthen you.

Abundance, in its truest sense, is not just about material wealth or success; it's about a mindset that believes that there is always more to learn, more to experience, and more to give. It's about feeling empowered, no matter what your external circumstances are. When you shift from despair to abundance, you open yourself up to the idea that life is full of potential, and you have the power to create your own path forward.

So, how do you begin this journey?

The first step is recognizing that **your current state is not your final destination.** Despair may feel permanent right now, but it is not a life sentence. It's a signal that something needs to change, that you are ready for growth. And just as seasons change, so can your mind, your heart, and your life.

Next, it's about **shifting the way you see yourself.** If you're stuck in despair, chances are you're viewing yourself through a lens of limitation—believing that you're not capable, not worthy, or not deserving of better things. The truth is, **you are deserving of every good thing that comes your way.** Abundance is not reserved for a lucky few—it's available to anyone willing to break free from limiting beliefs and step into their true power.

Part of the journey involves embracing gratitude. When you're in despair, it's easy to focus on what's going wrong or what you don't have. But the key to unlocking abundance lies in shifting your focus to the blessings, big and small, that are already in your life. Gratitude opens your heart and shifts your energy from lack to abundance, from fear to possibility. Start by looking for the things you're grateful for every single day. This simple practice will begin to change your vibration and open up new opportunities.

The journey to abundance also requires action. It's one thing to think positively and visualize success, but it's another to take tangible steps forward. Start small. Whether it's learning a new skill, reaching out for support, or simply showing up for yourself every day, each action you take will create momentum. And as you take action, you'll start to see results—results that reinforce your belief that you are capable of achieving more than you thought possible.

Lastly, **embrace the power of belief.** As you move forward on this journey, you'll start to see that your beliefs are the driving force behind everything you experience. When you believe in your ability to create change, you'll start to act like someone who is capable of success. And the more you act with confidence and clarity, the more the universe will align with your energy, presenting you with opportunities that once seemed impossible.

Remember, the journey from despair to abundance is not a straight path. There will be moments of doubt and fear along the way, but each step you take will move you closer to the life you're meant to live. This journey is about more than just changing your circumstances; it's about transforming the way you see yourself and the world around you. It's about moving from a place of scarcity and limitation to one of infinite possibility and growth.

As you take this journey, know that you are never alone. There is a vast, limitless source of strength within you that is just waiting to be tapped into. The abundance you seek is already within you, and every step you take toward change will reveal new levels of peace, joy, and fulfilment.

The journey ahead is yours to take. And with each step, you'll find yourself moving from despair to a life of true abundance. Your world is about to change—because you've chosen to change your mind.

How to Use this Book: A Practical Guide

Congratulations on beginning this transformative journey. The pages ahead are filled with powerful insights, tools, and exercises designed to help you shift your mindset and embrace a life of limitless possibilities. But in order to fully benefit from this book, it's important to approach it with intention, commitment, and a willingness to apply what you learn. This is not just a book to read—it's a guide to *live by*.

Here's how you can make the most of this journey and turn the lessons in these chapters into lasting change:

1. Commit to the Process

Change doesn't happen overnight. While it's tempting to rush through the chapters or skim through the sections, true transformation takes time. Commit to working through each chapter at your own pace, allowing yourself the time to absorb, reflect, and apply the ideas to your own life. Transformation happens when you take consistent, small steps, and this book is designed to guide you one step at a time.

Practical Tip: Set a goal to read one chapter per week. This will give you time to reflect, do the exercises, and integrate the lessons into your life. Remember, it's not about speed—it's about depth.

2. Reflect and Journal Regularly

At the end of each chapter, you'll find exercises, prompts, and action steps. Don't rush through them. Take the time to really *think* about the questions and write your answers down. Journaling is one of the most powerful tools for self-reflection and growth. By putting your thoughts on paper, you'll not only clarify your emotions and ideas but also make them more real and tangible.

Practical Tip: Keep a dedicated journal for this book. After each chapter, reflect on the exercises and record your feelings, insights, and any shifts you notice. This journal will become a powerful record of your progress, reminding you of how far you've come.

3. Challenge Your Limiting Beliefs

As you go through the chapters, you may notice certain beliefs or patterns that no longer serve you—thoughts like, "I can't do this" or "I'm not good enough." These are the mental barriers that hold you back from your true potential. Each chapter provides you with tools to identify and challenge these beliefs. Be honest with yourself and open to the idea that you can change these thought patterns.

Practical Tip: In the moments when self-doubt creeps in, refer back to the exercises in Chapter 1 and Chapter 3 where you reflect on your limiting beliefs. Use those exercises as a tool to reframe your thinking and shift toward a more empowering mindset.

4. Take Action—Even Small Steps Matter

Knowledge alone isn't enough to create change. It's the actions you take that will determine the results you experience. Each chapter provides practical steps to help you move forward, whether it's implementing new habits, practicing affirmations, or challenging negative self-talk. The key is consistency. Small, daily actions will eventually lead to big changes.

Practical Tip: Identify one action from each chapter that feels doable and start implementing it into your routine. For example, if Chapter 4 discusses overcoming fear, start by taking a small, manageable action that scares you.

Celebrate every victory, no matter how small, because each one is a step toward greater confidence and success.

5. Visualize Your Success

Visualization is a powerful tool to reinforce the limitless mindset you're developing. Imagine the person you want to become—the confident, courageous, positive version of yourself who is capable of anything. Visualizing this future self will not only help you stay motivated but will also align your subconscious mind with the goals you're working toward.

Practical Tip: Set aside a few minutes each day to visualize yourself living the life you want. Picture yourself overcoming challenges, succeeding in your goals, and radiating positivity. The more vivid and real you make this vision, the more your mind will start to believe it—and eventually, you'll begin to act in ways that align with that vision.

6. Be Patient and Compassionate with Yourself

Changing your mindset and rewiring your brain is a process, not an event. There will be days when you feel inspired and empowered, and there will be days when you struggle. That's okay. Don't expect perfection from yourself. Be patient and compassionate as you take these steps toward change. Every setback is a lesson, and every mistake is an opportunity to learn and grow.

Practical Tip: When you feel frustrated or discouraged, return to your journal. Remind yourself of the progress you've already made. Reflect on how far you've come and be proud of the effort you're putting in. Treat yourself with the same kindness you would offer a close friend.

7. Track Your Progress

As you continue on this journey, take note of the shifts you begin to experience. You might notice that you're more confident, more open to new opportunities, or that you handle stress in a different way. Celebrate these small wins and use them as motivation to keep going. Tracking your progress not only shows you how much you've grown, but it also reinforces your belief that change is possible.

Practical Tip: At the start of your journey, write down where you are emotionally, mentally, and physically. Revisit this entry every few weeks to measure your progress. Seeing your own growth will keep you motivated and focused on your ultimate goal.

By following this practical guide, you'll be able to transform the ideas in this book into a daily reality. The journey from limitation to limitless thinking is one of self-discovery, courage, and growth. You have everything you need to succeed, and by taking consistent action, you'll begin to see the abundant life that's waiting for you.

Remember, **this book is not just to read; it's to live.** So, dive in, do the work, and watch as your life begins to shift in ways you never thought possible. The power is in your hands.

1

From Darkness to Dawn – Where You Are

The Trap of Negative Thinking

Negative thinking is a silent, yet powerful force. It creeps into your mind slowly, like a shadow that seems harmless at first, but before you know it, it's covering everything. In fact, many of us don't even realize how deeply we've fallen into this trap. Negative thoughts become a way of life, a default setting we unconsciously return to. We believe them to be truths, not realizing they're often just patterns—habits of thinking that hold us back from living fully and embracing the possibilities in front of us.

When we think negatively, our minds tend to focus on what could go wrong. We imagine the worst-case scenario, or we replay past failures over and over again, convincing ourselves that we will never be able to change or achieve anything meaningful. We're often so consumed by fear, doubt, and worry that we forget about the abundant possibilities available to us. The trap of negative thinking keeps us stuck in a loop of self-doubt, where every step we take is clouded by the belief that we're not good enough, or that success is just out of reach.

It's easy to fall into this trap. After all, negative thinking can feel familiar. It might even feel safer, like a way to protect yourself from disappointment or failure. If you expect the worst, it's less painful when things don't go as planned. But here's the truth: Negative thinking doesn't protect you from failure. It prevents you from trying in the first place. It holds you back from taking action, from stepping into the unknown, and from exploring new opportunities. It keeps you tethered to a reality where you're constantly playing small.

Consider this: How often have you thought, "I can't do this" or "It's too late for me"? These thoughts are not facts—they are just the stories you've been telling yourself, often rooted in fear or past disappointments. And the more you repeat them, the stronger they become. Over time, these negative thoughts become a self-fulfilling prophecy. The more you believe you can't succeed, the less likely you are to take the steps needed to make it happen.

Negative thinking also affects your emotions. When you dwell on what's wrong or what could go wrong, you amplify feelings of anxiety, stress, and frustration. It's like feeding a fire that only grows larger the more you give it attention. These emotions then cloud your judgment, making it harder to see the opportunities that might actually lead you toward success. Instead, you become paralyzed by fear and overwhelmed by the weight of what feels like an impossible task.

The trap of negative thinking is insidious because it feels natural—it's easy to get caught in the cycle of worry, doubt, and pessimism. But in reality, this pattern of thinking is holding you back from living the life you're capable of. It's not only limiting your potential, but it's also preventing you from seeing the truth: **you are more capable, more resilient, and more powerful than your negative thoughts would have you believe.**

So, how do you escape this trap?

The first step is awareness. You have to recognize when you're thinking negatively. Often, these thoughts come so naturally that you don't even notice they're happening. Start paying attention to your inner dialogue. When you catch yourself thinking something like, "I'm not good enough" or "This is too hard," challenge it. Ask yourself, "Is this really true? What evidence do I have to support this thought?"

Once you become aware of your negative thinking, the next step is to reframe it. Instead of focusing on what could go wrong, try to shift your focus to what could go right. When you catch yourself thinking, "I'll never succeed," replace it with, "I may face challenges, but I have the ability to learn and grow through them." This simple shift in perspective can break the grip of negative thinking and open the door to new possibilities.

Finally, remember that overcoming negative thinking is a practice. It takes time, and it won't happen overnight. Be patient with yourself. Every time you challenge a negative thought or reframe a pessimistic belief, you're rewiring your brain for a more positive, limitless mindset.

By breaking free from the trap of negative thinking, you can start to see your life through a new lens—one where opportunities are abundant, and your potential is limitless. This is the first step toward your transformation, from darkness to dawn.

Why We Feel Stuck? – Understanding Limiting Beliefs

Have you ever felt like you're stuck in a rut, no matter how hard you try to move forward? Like there's something holding you back, even when you know you're capable of so much more? If you have, you're not alone. One of the biggest reasons we feel stuck in life is because of something called *limiting beliefs*— thoughts and beliefs that tell us what we can't do, who we can't be, or what we don't deserve.

Limiting beliefs are like invisible chains that keep us from reaching our full potential. They often form early in life, shaped by our experiences, the things we've been told, and the messages we've picked up from the world around us. Maybe someone once told you that you weren't good enough, or you weren't capable of achieving your dreams. Over time, those words can become a part of your thinking, even if they no longer serve you.

The problem with limiting beliefs is that we don't always realize we're holding onto them. They're sneaky. They show up as thoughts like, "I'll never be successful," "I'm not smart enough," or "People like me can't have the life I want." These beliefs keep us playing small and stop us from taking risks, stepping up, and going after what we really want. The truth is, these beliefs are not facts. They're just stories we've been telling ourselves.

Here's the good news: *you don't have to stay stuck*. Once you start to recognize these limiting beliefs, you can start to change them. You have the power to rewrite your story. The first step is awareness—knowing that these beliefs are there, even if they've been buried deep. Then, you can challenge them. Ask yourself: *Is this belief true? Where did it come from? Is it helping or hurting me?*

When you start to replace those old, limiting beliefs with empowering ones, everything changes. You'll find yourself taking bold steps, thinking bigger, and believing that you are capable of achieving your dreams. Remember: your mind is incredibly powerful, and when you start to believe in yourself, you can break free from the things that have been holding you back for far too long. It's time to let go of what's been keeping you stuck and embrace the limitless possibilities that are waiting for you.

Facing the Truth – Where Are You Right Now?

Before you can embark on any journey of transformation, personal growth, or limitless thinking, you must first face a fundamental question: *Where are you right now?*

This question is not about where you wish you were, or where you hope to be one day. It's about facing the present truth—an honest assessment of your current situation, mindset, and emotional state. Only by acknowledging where you are can you plot a course for where you want to go.

It's easy to get caught up in the noise of aspirations, distractions, or the false narratives we tell ourselves. We often create stories that protect us from facing the discomfort of the present. We might convince ourselves that we are closer to our goals than we actually are, or we may bury our struggles beneath optimism that isn't grounded in reality.

But the first step in changing your mind and, consequently, your world, is a fearless and authentic evaluation of the current moment. This is a crucial part of limitless thinking because it creates the foundation upon which your transformation can take root.

The Power of Truth in Transformation

Facing the truth about where you are is not a defeat—it is the most empowering act you can do for yourself. By accepting your starting point without judgment, you give yourself the clarity to make the necessary adjustments and decisions that will propel you forward. Ignoring or denying your truth is like trying to navigate a journey without understanding the landscape. You might end up lost, frustrated, and stagnant.

Think of your life as a map. Each decision, experience, and belief has helped shape the place you are right now. If you aren't aware of your current location, your ability to plot a meaningful and realistic course forward will be limited. When you face the truth of your present circumstances—whether they're full of achievements or filled with challenges—you are reclaiming your power.

Questions to Help You Face Your Truth

To begin the process of assessing where you are right now, ask yourself the following:

- **What are my current thoughts and beliefs?**

  Are they empowering me or limiting me?

- **How do I feel emotionally on a daily basis?**

  Am I carrying emotional weight from past experiences or embracing a mindset of growth?

- **What actions am I taking toward my goals?**

  Are they aligned with the life I desire to create, or are they simply habits that keep me stuck?

- **Where do I feel stuck or uncertain?**

  Are there areas in my life where I'm avoiding truth or change out of fear?

- **What do I truly want?**

  Not just what others expect of me, but what aligns with my authentic self and deepest desires?

The answers to these questions will give you a powerful snapshot of where you stand in this moment. It may feel uncomfortable, but it is an essential practice of self-awareness. The more honest you are with yourself, the clearer your path will become.

Embracing Your Current Reality

There is no shame in acknowledging that you're not exactly where you want to be—this is where growth begins. The key is to avoid self-criticism or judgment. Remember, facing your truth isn't about dwelling on shortcomings; it's about gaining the insight and perspective necessary to move forward.

Limitless thinking requires a radical acceptance of your present reality, free from the fog of denial or the pressure of unattainable perfection. Only when you let go of where you think you *should* be can you open the door to real, transformative change.

Embrace where you are, as it is the fertile ground from which limitless possibilities will grow. When you step into your truth, you step into your power.

The Importance of Awareness in Transformation

In the journey of transformation, awareness is the first and most crucial step. It is the lens through which we view the world, ourselves, and the endless possibilities that lie ahead. Without awareness, transformation is like navigating through fog—directionless and uncertain. It is only when we bring our attention to the present moment, to our thoughts, behaviors, and the patterns that shape our reality, that we unlock the potential for change.

At its core, awareness is the ability to recognize what is and what isn't working in our lives. It's about becoming conscious of our internal dialogue, our habits, and the beliefs that may have held us back for years. For example, if you find yourself trapped in a cycle of self-doubt or fear, awareness allows you to pause and identify these limiting thoughts before they dictate your actions. This simple act of recognizing the pattern is the first step in dismantling it.

Awareness also brings clarity to our goals and desires. Without it, we can easily become distracted or overwhelmed by external pressures. But when we are fully aware of what we want, why we want it, and how we are currently aligning (or misaligning) with that vision, we gain the clarity needed to make intentional, purposeful changes. In *Limitless Thinking*, we explore how your thoughts and mindset directly influence the world you create. To truly change your mind, you must first understand what thoughts and beliefs are limiting your potential and holding you back from becoming the person you are destined to be.

Furthermore, awareness is the bridge between your current reality and your desired future. It allows you to identify the gaps between where you are now and where you want to be. When you are aware of your strengths, weaknesses, opportunities, and threats, you can make informed decisions that will lead you toward transformation. This is true not just on an individual level but also within organizations and communities. Awareness of the challenges, patterns, and behaviors that perpetuate the status quo is what sparks innovation, change, and growth.

But awareness does not just stop at recognizing problems; it is also the key to recognizing solutions. The more aware we become of the resources, opportunities, and possibilities available to us, the more creative and resourceful we become in overcoming obstacles. When we shift from being reactive to proactive, from merely surviving to thriving, we are tapping into the power of awareness.

In this book, we will explore how to cultivate this essential skill of awareness, from mindfulness practices to reframing negative beliefs. The power to transform your life lies in your ability to shift your mindset, and that shift begins with becoming acutely aware of your thoughts, behaviors, and the patterns you have been living by. The truth is, once you are aware, you are no longer bound by the limitations of your past or present circumstances. Awareness opens the door to limitless possibilities, allowing you to truly change your mind and, in turn, change your world.

Practical Step: Journalling to Confront Your Current Mindset

One of the most powerful and practical tools for transforming your mindset is journaling. Writing down your thoughts, feelings, and experiences allows you to confront your current mindset head-on and gain clarity on the beliefs that may be limiting your growth. It provides a safe space for reflection, helping you identify patterns of thinking that you might not have otherwise noticed. By putting your thoughts on paper, you can better understand what drives you, what holds you back, and how to start shifting your perspective.

Journaling serves as a mirror for your inner world. Often, we go through life with certain beliefs and assumptions that we are not fully aware of. These subconscious thought patterns shape the way we see ourselves and the world around us, often without us realizing how much power they have over our actions. When you take the time to write, you create an opportunity to observe these thoughts, question their validity, and explore new ways of thinking.

To begin, set aside a few minutes each day to write. You don't need a fancy journal or a specific format—just a notebook and the willingness to explore your mind will do. Start by reflecting on your current mindset. Ask yourself questions like:

- *What beliefs do I hold about myself that may be limiting my growth?*

- *What thoughts keep recurring in my mind that might be holding me back from achieving my goals?*

- *What fears or doubts are controlling my actions or preventing me from taking risks?*

Write freely and without judgment. The purpose here isn't to critique yourself but to bring these hidden beliefs into the light. You'll be surprised at what comes up when you allow yourself to express your inner dialogue without filtering it. In doing so, you may uncover negative self-talk, unproductive habits, or outdated beliefs that no longer serve you.

Once you've identified these thoughts, take the time to reflect on them. Are they rooted in truth, or are they simply fear-based reactions or societal conditioning? Challenge these thoughts by asking yourself:

- *Is this belief really true?*

- *How does this belief limit me, and how would my life be different if I changed it?*

- *What new beliefs or thoughts can I adopt to support my growth and transformation?*

Rewriting your mindset starts by consciously replacing negative or limiting thoughts with more empowering alternatives. Journaling gives you the space to practice this cognitive shift. Over time, as you write, you'll find that you naturally begin to adopt a new perspective on yourself and the world around you.

One helpful exercise is to write in your journal about a situation where you felt stuck or overwhelmed. Describe the event, and then explore the mindset that led to that feeling. What were you thinking in that moment? What beliefs were influencing your actions? Then, reframe the situation by writing a new narrative, one where you respond from a place of confidence and possibility. This exercise can help you rewire your brain to view challenges as opportunities rather than obstacles.

Journaling also helps you track your progress over time. By revisiting previous entries, you can see how far you've come and recognize the changes in your mindset. This ongoing practice not only increases self-awareness but also fosters a deeper connection to your personal transformation.

In *Limitless Thinking*, we discuss how your thoughts create your reality. Journaling is one of the most effective ways to begin consciously changing those thoughts. By confronting your current mindset, understanding the beliefs that may be holding you back, and replacing them with thoughts that empower you, journaling becomes an essential tool in transforming your mind—and ultimately, your world.

2

The Power of Choice – Shifting the Lens

How Your Thoughts are Shaping Your World

Your thoughts are not just fleeting, abstract concepts—they are the architects of your reality. Every thought you have is a building block, shaping your perceptions, influencing your actions, and creating the world you experience. This is the essence of the power of choice: you have the ability to choose your thoughts, and in doing so, you shape the lens through which you see the world. Understanding this is the first step toward true transformation.

At the most basic level, the way you think directly impacts how you interpret and respond to the world around you. For example, if you approach a challenging situation with a mindset of fear or doubt, your actions will likely reflect that energy. You may avoid taking risks, hesitate in making decisions, or feel overwhelmed by obstacles. On the other hand, if you approach the same situation with a mindset of possibility and resilience, you're more likely to face challenges head-on, look for solutions, and embrace opportunities for growth.

Your thoughts create a filter that colors your perception of reality. Think of it like wearing glasses with a specific tint. If your glasses are tinted with negativity, everything you see will seem dark or discouraging. If your glasses are tinted with optimism, even in the face of adversity, you'll find the silver lining and seek ways to make progress. This lens of perception influences how you engage with others, how you view your goals, and how you respond to setbacks.

The power of choice comes in when you realize that you have the ability to change the lens through which you view your life. While you can't always control what happens to you, you have full control over how you choose to think about those events. It's important to recognize that the thoughts you hold most frequently—your core beliefs and self-talk—are the foundation upon which your experiences are built.

For instance, consider your thoughts about success. If you believe that success is difficult to achieve and only for a select few, this belief will shape your actions, and you may avoid pursuing your dreams because you feel it's out of reach. But if you shift that belief to one of possibility, where you see success as a result of consistent effort, resilience, and learning, your behavior will change. You'll take more risks, push through challenges, and open yourself to new opportunities. In this way, the lens you choose to view the world through directly influences the reality you create.

The beauty of this understanding lies in the fact that you have the power to change your thoughts at any moment. This is where the idea of shifting the lens comes into play. When you become aware of your thought patterns—especially the ones that limit you—you can consciously choose to reframe them. For example, if you think, *"I'm not good enough to succeed,"* you can challenge this thought by shifting it to, *"I am capable of learning and growing through my experiences."* With each shift, you begin to rewire your brain to see more opportunities and embrace challenges with confidence rather than fear.

Your thoughts also influence your emotions, which in turn impact your actions. If you constantly think negative, self-critical thoughts, you may feel discouraged, anxious, or unmotivated. These emotions then affect the choices you make, often leading to inaction or self-sabotage. On the other hand, when you choose empowering thoughts—thoughts that focus on your potential and resilience— you feel motivated, confident, and focused. This shift in mindset leads to empowered action and, ultimately, a transformed life.

In *Limitless Thinking*, we delve deeper into the transformative power of choosing your thoughts. When you recognize that your thoughts shape your reality, you understand that the key to changing your world begins with changing how you think. By consciously shifting your mindset, you shift the lens through which you view yourself and the world. And as your perspective changes, so too does the world you create. The power of choice lies in the awareness that you can choose a new thought at any moment—and in doing so, you can begin to shape a new world, one thought at a time.

Breaking Free from Victimhood

One of the most powerful steps you can take in your journey toward transformation is breaking free from the mindset of victimhood. The victim mentality is a state of mind where you believe that circumstances, people, or external forces control your life. It's a mindset that leaves you feeling powerless, trapped, and often resigned to a life of frustration or limitation. When you see yourself as a victim, you give away your power, believing that things are happening to you rather than for you.

But here's the truth: *You are not a victim of your circumstances.* No matter what has happened in your past, you have the power to choose how you respond and how you move forward. Breaking free from victimhood starts with recognizing that you are the author of your own story, and you have the ability to change the narrative at any time.

The first step in breaking free from victimhood is becoming aware of the thoughts and beliefs that reinforce it. Do you often tell yourself things like, *"This always happens to me,"* or *"I can't catch a break"*? These thoughts are rooted in the belief that you have no control over your circumstances and that life is happening to you in a way that you can't change. This mindset keeps you stuck in a cycle of helplessness and disempowerment.

But the reality is that the power to transform your life lies within you. You may not be able to change everything about your past or current circumstances, but you always have the power to choose how you react. This shift in mindset—from being a passive victim to becoming an active participant in your life—is the key to unlocking your true potential.

Start by asking yourself empowering questions, such as:

- *What can I learn from this situation?*

- *How can I grow from this challenge?*

- *What steps can I take right now to shift my situation?*

These questions shift your focus from what is out of your control to what you can control: your thoughts, actions, and responses. By adopting this mindset, you begin to see challenges as opportunities for growth rather than insurmountable obstacles. Every setback becomes a chance to learn, evolve, and take charge of your own life.

Another key to breaking free from victimhood is taking full responsibility for your actions, thoughts, and feelings. This doesn't mean blaming yourself for everything that has happened to you, but rather recognizing that you are the one who has the power to change how you perceive and respond to the world. When you take responsibility for your reactions, you take back your power. Instead of waiting for others or circumstances to change, you realize that the real change begins with you.

It's also important to let go of the need to blame others for your struggles. When you hold onto anger, resentment, or the belief that someone or something else is to blame for your situation, you remain stuck in the past, unable to move forward. Forgiveness is not just for others—it's for you. Releasing blame allows you to free yourself from the grip of victimhood and step into a place of empowerment and possibility.

Breaking free from victimhood also involves shifting your focus from what's wrong to what's right. When you focus solely on the negative, it becomes your reality. But when you start to look for the positives—however small they may seem—you begin to see the world in a different light. Practicing gratitude and shifting your focus to what you do have, rather than what you don't, can radically change the way you experience life.

Finally, breaking free from victimhood requires the courage to take action. It's easy to feel stuck when you believe that you are powerless, but the truth is, action is one of the most empowering things you can do. It doesn't have to be a giant leap—small steps forward are enough to create momentum. Each time you take action, you reinforce the belief that you have control over your life and your future. And with each step, you become more confident in your ability to create change.

We explore how breaking free from victimhood is a vital part of reclaiming your personal power and moving toward a life of limitless possibilities. By shifting from a mindset of victimhood to one of empowerment, you choose to take ownership of your life, your decisions, and your future. This shift allows you to move from feeling helpless to becoming the creator of your own reality. The world around you may not always change, but when you change your mindset and your actions, you begin to shape a new, more powerful version of yourself. And that is where true transformation begins.

Recognizing the Power of Choice in Every Moment

In every moment, you stand at a crossroads, holding the key to shaping your future. The power of choice is the most fundamental force in your life, yet it is often the most overlooked. We tend to think of our choices as a reaction to the world around us—situations that just "happen" to us, circumstances beyond our control. But what if I told you that in every interaction, in every challenge, and even in the most mundane moments, you have the power to choose? Not just your actions, but your thoughts, your attitude, and your perspective.

The power of choice is not about what happens to you; it's about how you choose to respond. Life is full of unexpected twists, setbacks, and challenges. While you can't always control external circumstances, you can always choose how to navigate them. The real magic lies in recognizing that, at every given moment, you hold the ability to decide how you show up in the world. This is the foundation of personal transformation: the awareness that *you* are in charge of your reactions, your mindset, and ultimately, your life's direction.

Take a moment to reflect on the times when you felt powerless. Maybe you were stuck in a situation that seemed unchangeable, or you faced a setback that felt like a roadblock. In those moments, did you know that you still had the power to choose your response? It may not have felt like it then, but in retrospect, you had a choice. You could have chosen to stay in a place of victimhood, to blame others or circumstances for your troubles. Or, you could have chosen to embrace resilience, to see the challenge as an opportunity to learn and grow.

The difference between those two paths lies in one simple yet profound concept: *choice*. Your choice of thoughts, actions, and attitudes shapes your reality. In *Limitless Thinking*, I emphasize that the external world is often a reflection of our internal world. If you approach life with a mindset that sees challenges as insurmountable obstacles, that's exactly how they will feel. But if you choose to see challenges as stepping stones for growth, as opportunities for learning, that's how they will unfold.

What makes this realization so powerful is that you're not waiting for permission or for things to change. You don't need the world to align perfectly for you to create a life you love. You already possess the power of choice, right here and right now. It's in how you approach your work, your relationships, and even your personal growth. When you recognize this power, you stop waiting for the perfect moment and begin to create it yourself.

The beauty of choice is that it is not just reserved for big, life-altering decisions. It lives in the everyday moments. Every time you wake up, you have the choice of how you want to begin your day. Will you choose to start with gratitude, with intention, with focus? Or will you allow the chaos of the world to dictate your mood and actions? Every interaction with another person is a choice—will you choose kindness, understanding, and patience, or will you react with frustration and defensiveness? Even in moments of difficulty, you have the choice of how to respond—will you choose resilience or despair?

This power of choice is what shifts your perspective from being a passive observer of life to an active creator of your own reality. And the more consciously you choose, the more empowered you become. You realize that you are not at the mercy of your circumstances; you are the creator of your experience. Every small choice adds up, shaping the larger patterns of your life.

But here's the key: You must first become aware of the choices you're making. Often, we fall into unconscious patterns of thinking and reacting. We allow fear, old beliefs, and automatic responses to drive us. But when you truly understand the power of choice, you begin to step into each moment with full awareness and intention. You choose thoughts that serve you. You choose actions that align with your highest potential. And you choose attitudes that empower you to navigate the world with confidence and grace.

It's important to recognize that the power of choice does not mean that life will always be easy or perfect. You will still face challenges, setbacks, and difficult moments. But when you recognize that you have the power to choose how you respond to them, you stop being a victim of your circumstances and start becoming the creator of your life. You realize that *you* hold the pen, and you can rewrite your story at any moment.

In *Limitless Thinking*, we explore how understanding the power of choice transforms not just how you think, but how you live. You are the author of your own life, and in every moment, you have the power to choose the next chapter. The true magic of life is realizing that your choices are limitless, and in those choices lies the power to create the world you've always dreamed of. It all starts with recognizing this one simple truth: The power of choice is in your hands—always.

Shifting Your Perspective: Seeing Possibility Instead of Failure

---

One of the most transformative shifts you can make in your life is changing the way you view failure. Our culture often teaches us to fear failure, to see it as something to avoid at all costs. We've been conditioned to believe that failing means we're not good enough, that we're incapable, or that we're somehow lacking. But the truth is, failure is not the opposite of success—*it is part of the process of success*. In order to break free from this limiting belief, you must shift your perspective. Instead of seeing failure as something to be feared, you must begin to see it as a stepping stone to possibility.

This shift begins with the recognition that your perspective shapes your reality. How you view challenges, setbacks, and mistakes directly influences how you respond to them. If you look at failure as a permanent defeat, it will discourage you from moving forward. But if you shift your perspective to see failure as a valuable lesson and a necessary part of growth, you will embrace each setback as an opportunity to learn, adapt, and get closer to your goal.

Think about it: every successful person, every trailblazer, every visionary has faced failure. They've experienced the crushing disappointment of setbacks, the sting of rejection, and the frustration of things not going as planned. But what sets them apart is not that they didn't fail—it's that they refused to let failure define them. Instead of seeing failure as an endpoint, they saw it as a valuable part of their journey, one that provided insight, clarity, and ultimately, growth.

The key to shifting your perspective is to reframe the way you define failure. Failure isn't a reflection of your worth or your abilities—it's a natural part of learning and evolving. The real failure lies in giving up, in quitting before you've given yourself the chance to grow. If you approach failure as a lesson rather than a verdict, you'll start to see every mistake as a chance to improve. Each time you fall short, you gain information about what works and what doesn't, what you need to adjust, and what you need to try next.

In *Limitless Thinking*, we explore how failure is often the greatest teacher. It forces you to stretch beyond your comfort zone, to break through self-imposed limits, and to approach challenges with a new mindset. Instead of asking, *"Why did I fail?"* ask yourself, *"What can I learn from this experience?"* When you shift your focus from what went wrong to what you can gain, you begin to see every setback as an opportunity for growth.

Another important aspect of shifting your perspective is recognizing that failure doesn't define your future. Too often, we carry the weight of past failures with us, allowing them to influence our confidence and limit our potential. But your past mistakes don't dictate your future success unless you allow them to. Every moment is a new opportunity, a blank canvas for you to create the life you desire.

By focusing on possibility instead of failure, you open yourself up to a world of opportunities that would have been previously blocked by fear and doubt. When you see every challenge as a chance to grow and improve, you begin to take more risks, make bolder decisions, and step outside of your comfort zone. With this mindset, you begin to see life as a playground for growth rather than a series of obstacles.

Shifting your perspective also requires a commitment to reframing the way you see success. Success isn't about never failing—it's about failing forward. It's about continuing to move toward your goals, even when things don't go as planned. The path to success is rarely linear. It's full of twists, turns, and detours. But each of these moments, even the difficult ones, brings you closer to where you want to be. When you embrace the process and see failure as a natural part of the journey, you'll find that success comes not in spite of your setbacks, but because of them.

Remember, the only true failure is not trying at all. The fear of failure often holds us back from taking action, from stepping into our greatness. But when you shift your perspective and begin to see failure as nothing more than a temporary setback, you release the fear that keeps you stuck. You free yourself to take bold, decisive action—knowing that every experience, no matter how challenging, is a valuable piece of your growth.

In the end, the ability to see possibility instead of failure is a game-changer. It allows you to approach life with curiosity, resilience, and confidence. Instead of fearing what might go wrong, you begin to focus on what might go right. You begin to trust the process and recognize that every setback is simply a stepping stone to your ultimate success.

When you shift your perspective, you shift your reality. You stop seeing obstacles as barriers and start seeing them as opportunities to grow stronger, smarter, and more capable. And in doing so, you unlock a limitless future, where failure is not a dead end, but a launchpad for your next big breakthrough.

Practical Step: Rewriting Your Story – Affirmations for Change

One of the most powerful tools for transforming your mindset and rewriting the narrative of your life is the practice of affirmations. Affirmations are positive, empowering statements that you repeat to yourself to challenge and change the limiting beliefs that may be holding you back. They are not just words; they are seeds you plant in your mind, seeds that grow into new beliefs and, ultimately, a new reality.

The stories we tell ourselves shape our lives. From a young age, we internalize messages about who we are, what we can achieve, and what is possible for us. These stories, often influenced by our experiences, societal expectations, and the opinions of others, become deeply ingrained in our subconscious minds. Over time, they can dictate our behavior, limit our potential, and keep us from stepping into the greatness we are capable of.

But here's the good news: you have the power to change your story at any moment. The key is recognizing that the thoughts and beliefs you hold about yourself are not fixed truths; they are simply stories you've been telling yourself. And just like any story, you can rewrite it. This is where affirmations come in— they are the tool you can use to consciously create a new narrative, one that empowers you to become the person you want to be and to achieve the things you want to achieve.

The process of using affirmations begins with identifying the limiting beliefs that are holding you back. These are often the thoughts that sound something like: *"I'm not good enough," "I don't deserve success,"* or *"I'll never be able to do this."* These beliefs are powerful because they shape your actions and influence how you show up in the world. But they are not the truth—they are simply the product of your past experiences and conditioning.

Once you've identified these limiting beliefs, you can replace them with empowering affirmations that reflect the version of yourself you want to become. For example, if you've been telling yourself, *"I'm not capable,"* you can rewrite that story with an affirmation like, *"I am capable of achieving anything I set my mind to."* If your belief is, *"I don't deserve success,"* reframe it to, *"I am worthy of success and abundance in every area of my life."*

The key to effective affirmations is to make them present, positive, and personal. Instead of focusing on what you don't want (e.g., *"I don't want to fail"*), focus on what you *do* want (e.g., *"I am successful in everything I do."*). Make the affirmation specific to your goals and use language that feels authentic to you. It's important that when you say the affirmation, you truly believe it and feel it in your heart.

To make affirmations a practical part of your life, integrate them into your daily routine. You can say them out loud in front of the mirror, write them down in your journal, or even record them and listen to them throughout the day. The more frequently you repeat your affirmations, the more you will reprogram your subconscious mind. Over time, these positive statements will begin to replace the old, limiting beliefs, and your new story will start to take root.

An example of a daily affirmation practice could look like this:

- **Morning:** Start your day by saying a series of affirmations that set the tone for your day: *"Today, I am confident and capable. I approach every challenge with optimism. I trust in my ability to create success."*

- **Midday:** If you encounter a challenge or a moment of self-doubt, take a pause and repeat a calming affirmation: *"I am resilient, and I have everything I need to handle this situation."*

- **Night:** Before bed, reflect on your day and affirm your progress: *"I am proud of the steps I took today. I am becoming the person I've always wanted to be."*

Incorporating affirmations into your daily life is a simple but profoundly effective way to begin rewriting your story. It may feel awkward or unnatural at first, but with consistency and intention, you'll begin to notice a shift in your thoughts, your actions, and your outcomes. Affirmations help you build a new mental framework—one that empowers you to break free from limiting beliefs and step into the life you deserve.

Remember, your thoughts create your reality. By using affirmations, you take control of your inner dialogue, shifting it from one of doubt and fear to one of possibility and empowerment. And as your internal narrative changes, so too will the world around you.

In *Limitless Thinking*, we explore how rewiring your thoughts and beliefs is essential to breaking free from self-imposed limitations and unlocking your full potential. Affirmations are a practical tool that, when used consistently, can help you create a new story—one that reflects the limitless possibilities within you. By consciously rewriting your story with empowering words, you step into your power and begin to create the life you've always dreamed of.

3

The Neuroscience of Limitless Thinking

Understanding How Your Brain Works

To truly understand how to rewire your brain and unlock the power of limitless thinking, it helps to first understand the basics of how your brain works. While it may seem complex, the brain is actually designed to help you succeed—it just needs the right guidance. Once you know how to tap into its natural abilities, you can start to shift your mindset and rewire the patterns that have been holding you back.

Your brain is like a super-powered computer, constantly processing information and making decisions based on past experiences, emotions, and beliefs. The key to transforming your thinking is realizing that your brain is highly adaptable—this is a concept called **neuroplasticity**. Neuroplasticity is the brain's ability to change and reorganize itself, forming new neural connections throughout your life. This means that you're not stuck with the patterns and habits you have right now. No matter how deeply ingrained a belief or behavior is, you have the power to change it with the right tools and mindset.

Think of your brain as a vast network of roads. Each thought you have is like a car driving down one of those roads. The more you think a certain thought, the more you reinforce the path, making it easier for the car to travel down that road in the future. Over time, some of these roads become highways—meaning, they are well-worn paths your brain naturally goes to without much effort. These highways represent your habits, thought patterns, and beliefs.

Now, here's the exciting part: just like you can create new roads in a city, you can create new neural pathways in your brain. When you start to think new thoughts, challenge old beliefs, and take new actions, you begin to carve new paths. At first, these roads might be bumpy and difficult to travel, but with repetition, they become smoother and easier to navigate. Eventually, these new roads can become just as powerful as the old ones—and in some cases, even stronger.

For example, let's say you have a habit of thinking *"I'm not good enough"* whenever faced with a challenge. This thought has likely been reinforced over time, creating a well-worn neural pathway in your brain. But if you begin to consciously challenge that thought and replace it with something empowering, like *"I am capable and I have the skills to handle this,"* you start to carve a new pathway. In the beginning, it may feel awkward, and you might even slip back into the old pattern of thinking. But with consistent effort, this new belief becomes more natural, and the old, limiting belief loses its power.

The more you practice positive thinking, the more you strengthen these new neural pathways. Eventually, your brain will begin to default to these empowering thoughts, and your perception of yourself and your abilities will shift. This is how you rewire your brain for limitless thinking.

Another important aspect of understanding how your brain works is recognizing the role of emotions. Your brain is not just logical—it is deeply emotional, and emotions play a huge role in shaping your thoughts and behaviors. When you experience an emotion, your brain releases chemicals that either reinforce positive feelings (like joy and excitement) or negative ones (like fear and anxiety). The brain doesn't differentiate between real or imagined threats—it simply reacts to how you feel. This means that your thoughts and emotions are constantly interacting with each other, creating a feedback loop that reinforces certain beliefs and patterns.

For instance, if you constantly think about what could go wrong, your brain interprets that as a threat and floods your body with stress hormones. This creates a feeling of fear, which in turn makes you more likely to act in ways that reinforce that fear (perhaps by avoiding challenges or opportunities). On the other hand, when you focus on positive outcomes, possibility, and excitement, your brain releases feel-good chemicals like dopamine and serotonin, reinforcing feelings of confidence and motivation.

By understanding how your brain processes emotions and thoughts, you can begin to consciously choose which emotions you want to amplify. If you want to create a mindset of limitless thinking, you need to focus on cultivating positive emotions, such as gratitude, joy, and excitement. These positive emotions help rewire your brain by creating neural connections that support your growth and success.

Finally, one of the most powerful tools in rewiring your brain is mindfulness. Mindfulness is the practice of being present and aware of your thoughts, feelings, and actions without judgment. When you practice mindfulness, you gain greater control over your thoughts and emotions, allowing you to break free from old patterns and create new ones. Mindfulness helps you become more aware of your automatic reactions, giving you the opportunity to choose a different response— one that aligns with your vision of limitless thinking.

Understanding how your brain works is the first step in taking control of your thoughts, emotions, and actions. When you embrace the concept of neuroplasticity, you realize that your brain is not fixed—it's malleable, adaptable, and ready for change. You are not defined by your past beliefs or current circumstances. By consciously choosing to think differently, feel differently, and act differently, you begin to rewire your brain, paving the way for a new, limitless version of yourself. The power to change is within you—and it all starts with understanding how your brain works.

Neuroplasticity: The Brain's Ability to Change

Neuroplasticity is one of the most exciting discoveries in the field of neuroscience. It's the brain's remarkable ability to reorganize itself by forming new neural connections throughout your life. Think of it like the brain's way of saying, *"I'm not stuck—I can change and adapt."* This is incredibly empowering because it means that no matter how old you are or how long you've been stuck in a certain pattern of thinking or behavior, your brain has the capacity to change. And the best part? You have the power to guide that change.

Imagine your brain as a vast network of highways. Every thought you have, every habit you form, creates a new pathway. The more you think a particular thought or perform a specific action, the stronger that pathway becomes. Over time, these pathways turn into deeply ingrained habits or beliefs that shape your experience of the world. But the beauty of neuroplasticity is that even well-established pathways are not set in stone. You can pave new routes, create fresh connections, and change the way your brain works.

For example, if you've always believed that you're not good enough, your brain has formed a well-worn pathway that reinforces that belief. Every time you encounter a challenge, your mind might automatically go to thoughts like, *"I can't do this"* or *"I'm not smart enough."* But through neuroplasticity, you can start forming new pathways that reflect a more empowering belief. By consistently choosing to think differently—by intentionally telling yourself, *"I am capable,"* or *"I have the skills to succeed"*— your brain starts to form new neural connections that support this more positive, empowering belief.

The more you practice positive thinking, the more these new pathways become reinforced. At first, it might feel awkward or forced, like driving on a bumpy, unfamiliar road. But over time, with repetition, the new pathway becomes smoother and easier to navigate, and the old, limiting pathways lose their strength. Eventually, your new beliefs become second nature, and your brain shifts toward a more positive, confident way of thinking.

Neuroplasticity isn't just about changing your thoughts—it's also about changing your actions. The brain's ability to adapt and grow means that when you take new actions, try new things, or face new challenges, you create new pathways. Let's say you've been avoiding public speaking out of fear or anxiety. Each time you let that fear control you, your brain reinforces the pathway of avoidance. But if you choose to confront your fear—by speaking in front of a small group or practicing in front of a mirror—you create a new, empowering pathway. With each step, you strengthen the neural connections that make public speaking feel easier, until it becomes less intimidating and more natural.

This process of rewiring your brain is ongoing. Neuroplasticity doesn't stop once you've learned something new or changed a behavior—it's a lifelong process. Your brain is constantly adapting and forming new connections, and you can use this to your advantage by choosing to learn, grow, and expand in new ways throughout your life.

The key to harnessing neuroplasticity is to engage in practices that promote growth and change. These can include:

- **Mindfulness and Meditation:** These practices help you become more aware of your thoughts, which is the first step in changing them. By observing your thought patterns without judgment, you create space for new, more positive patterns to emerge.

- **Learning New Skills:** Whether it's learning a new language, taking up a new hobby, or challenging yourself in your work, learning something new stimulates neuroplasticity by forcing your brain to make new connections.

- **Positive Affirmations:** Repeating positive affirmations helps rewire the brain by reinforcing new beliefs and behaviors. The more consistently you affirm your capabilities and potential, the stronger the neural pathways become that support those beliefs.

- **Physical Exercise:** Exercise is not only good for the body—it's great for the brain as well. It increases the production of brain-derived neurotrophic factor (BDNF), a protein that encourages the growth and repair of neurons, supporting neuroplasticity.

The more you practice these activities, the more you create the conditions for your brain to thrive and grow. Just like lifting weights strengthens muscles, consistently engaging in brain-boosting practices strengthens the neural pathways that support a limitless mindset.

Neuroplasticity offers hope, flexibility, and freedom. It reminds us that we are not prisoners of our past habits or thoughts. The brain's adaptability means that you are always capable of growth and transformation. By understanding and harnessing the power of neuroplasticity, you can change your mindset, improve your habits, and unlock the potential that lies within you.

The ability to rewire your brain means that you are not defined by your past experiences or limiting beliefs. You can create new patterns of thinking, act in ways that align with your true potential, and cultivate a life of limitless possibility. So, if you've ever felt like change is impossible, let neuroplasticity be your reminder: You can change. You can grow. And you can create the life you've always dreamed of.

The Impact of Repetition and New Habits

When it comes to rewiring your brain and creating lasting change, repetition and new habits are the keys to success. The brain is like a muscle—it strengthens with consistent use. Every time you repeat a behavior, thought, or action, your brain forms a stronger neural connection, making that behavior or thought easier and more automatic. This is why repetition is so crucial in the process of transformation. It's the practice that turns new ideas into new realities.

Habits are the foundation of our daily lives. In fact, most of our actions—around 40-45% of them—are driven by habits, not conscious decision-making. Whether it's the way we brush our teeth, the foods we eat, or how we react to stress, our brain has created pathways for these habits over time. The more we repeat something, the more ingrained the habit becomes, and the more automatic it feels.

This is the core principle behind creating positive change: the brain is wired to repeat what it is familiar with. So, if you want to shift from old, limiting behaviors to empowering ones, the key is consistency. When you consciously choose to repeat a new, positive habit, your brain begins to form new pathways, reinforcing the behavior until it becomes second nature.

Let's break this down with a simple example: Imagine you want to start exercising regularly. At first, it might feel hard, and the brain will resist because it's not a familiar path. The neural pathway for exercising isn't fully formed yet, so it takes effort to make the choice, put on your workout clothes, and actually get moving. But with each repetition, you are laying down a new road. The more often you exercise, the easier it gets. Over time, your brain begins to view exercise as a natural, automatic behavior. The effort required to get started diminishes, and eventually, it becomes a regular part of your day.

The science behind this is fascinating. When you repeat a behavior, your brain releases dopamine, the "feel-good" neurotransmitter. Dopamine acts like a reward, reinforcing the habit and motivating you to continue. As you experience small victories along the way, like feeling stronger after a workout or noticing positive changes in your body, your brain learns to associate that behavior with positive outcomes. The more you repeat the behavior, the more the neural pathways become reinforced, and the habit becomes ingrained.

However, it's important to understand that not all repetition is equal. Simply repeating something isn't enough—how you repeat it matters. To create lasting change, you need to focus on **intentional repetition**. This means being fully engaged and mindful of the process, not just going through the motions. When you are fully present while creating a new habit—whether it's exercising, practicing gratitude, or learning something new—you activate the brain's prefrontal cortex, which is responsible for higher-order thinking, decision-making, and planning. This allows you to create more deliberate and lasting neural changes.

Another important factor is patience. Creating new habits and reinforcing them through repetition takes time. It's easy to become discouraged if you don't see immediate results, but remember that transformation is a process. Research suggests that, on average, it takes around 66 days to form a new habit, but this can vary depending on the complexity of the behavior and your level of commitment. The key is to keep showing up, even on the days when you don't feel like it. Each small, consistent step moves you closer to making that new habit automatic.

The good news is that your brain is incredibly adaptable. If you've been stuck in a cycle of unproductive or negative habits, it's never too late to change. The brain's neuroplasticity means that you can form new, positive habits at any age, no matter how long you've been stuck in your old ways. Repetition is the tool that allows you to override old patterns and create new, empowering ones.

When you combine repetition with conscious intention, you start to create a life built on habits that serve your highest potential. Instead of reacting to life based on old, automatic behaviors, you begin to make decisions that align with your goals and vision for the future. Over time, these new habits create a ripple effect, improving your mindset, your health, your relationships, and your success.

So, whether you're working on developing a new mindset, learning a new skill, or improving your daily routine, repetition is your ally. Remember, the more you repeat the behaviors and thoughts that align with the person you want to become, the more you will strengthen the neural pathways that support those behaviors. The brain is your most powerful tool—use repetition wisely, and it will help you turn your aspirations into reality. With consistent effort and patience, you'll find that what once felt difficult or unnatural becomes effortless and ingrained in who you are.

How to Start Rewiring Your Brain for Positivity

Rewiring your brain for positivity is not a one-time fix—it's a process that requires commitment and consistent effort. The good news is, your brain is incredibly adaptable and capable of change, no matter how deeply ingrained negative thought patterns might feel. By understanding how your brain works and taking small, purposeful steps, you can start shifting your mindset toward more positive, empowering thoughts. Here's how to begin:

1. Become Aware of Your Thoughts

The first step in rewiring your brain for positivity is awareness. Most of us are unaware of how often we engage in negative self-talk or pessimistic thinking. But by simply paying attention to your thoughts, you can start to notice patterns of negativity. Are you often thinking, *"I'm not good enough,"* or *"This will never work"*? These negative thoughts are like grooves in your brain that you've created over time. The more aware you become of these patterns, the easier it is to catch them and choose a new path.

To start, try keeping a thought journal. Throughout the day, jot down the negative thoughts that pop into your mind. This will give you clarity on what's going on in your head, and from there, you can begin the process of changing them.

2. Challenge Negative Thoughts with Reframing

Once you become aware of your negative thoughts, the next step is to challenge them. When you think, *"I can't do this,"* ask yourself, *"What's the evidence for this thought? What if I could do it, or at least try?"* Reframing is the practice of seeing a situation from a different perspective. Instead of focusing on what's wrong, ask yourself what's right, or how you can turn the challenge into an opportunity.

For example, if you're faced with a difficult project at work, rather than thinking, *"This is too hard, I'll never finish it,"* reframe it as, *"This is an opportunity to learn something new, and I'll tackle it step by step."* Over time, reframing helps your brain start to look for solutions and possibilities instead of focusing on problems and limitations.

3. Practice Gratitude Daily

Gratitude is a powerful tool for rewiring your brain for positivity. When you focus on what you're thankful for, your brain releases feel-good chemicals like dopamine and serotonin, which improve mood and overall well-being. The more you practice gratitude, the more your brain starts to look for things to appreciate, instead of dwelling on what's lacking.

A simple way to start is to write down three things you're grateful for each day. These don't have to be big or grand; even the small moments matter. It could be as simple as being grateful for a good cup of coffee, a kind gesture from a friend, or the beauty of nature. The key is consistency—making gratitude a daily habit helps train your brain to focus on abundance, not scarcity.

4. Use Positive Affirmations

Positive affirmations are statements that challenge limiting beliefs and reinforce empowering thoughts. These simple yet powerful statements help reprogram your subconscious mind. When you repeat affirmations such as, *"I am worthy of success,"* or *"I am capable of handling challenges,"* you start to overwrite the negative self-talk and replace it with beliefs that empower you.

Start by identifying areas in your life where you feel insecure or doubtful. Write down affirmations that address those areas. For example, if you struggle with self-doubt, use affirmations like, *"I trust myself,"* or *"I am confident in my abilities."* Repeat your affirmations daily, ideally in the morning or before bed, when your mind is more receptive to new beliefs.

5. Engage in Mindfulness and Meditation

Mindfulness and meditation are powerful tools to help shift your mindset toward positivity. Mindfulness involves being fully present in the moment, observing your thoughts and feelings without judgment. Meditation, particularly mindfulness meditation, helps you quiet the mind, reduce stress, and cultivate a positive mindset.

Start by dedicating just 5–10 minutes a day to mindfulness or meditation. You can sit quietly, focus on your breath, and gently bring your attention back to the present moment whenever your mind wanders. Over time, these practices will help you become less reactive to negative thoughts and more capable of cultivating a calm, positive mindset.

6. Surround Yourself with Positivity

The people and environments around you have a powerful influence on your mindset. If you want to rewire your brain for positivity, start surrounding yourself with positive influences. This could mean spending more time with supportive and uplifting people, consuming media that inspires and motivates you, or creating a physical environment that makes you feel happy and peaceful.

Your brain is constantly absorbing information from your surroundings. By consciously choosing positivity—whether it's in the form of uplifting books, inspiring podcasts, or spending time with people who encourage and support you—you create an environment that nurtures a positive mindset.

7. Celebrate Small Wins

Rewiring your brain takes time, so it's important to acknowledge and celebrate your progress along the way. Each time you catch a negative thought and replace it with something more positive, or when you stick to a new habit like gratitude or affirmation practice, give yourself credit. Celebrating small wins reinforces the idea that you're making progress, which motivates you to continue.

This doesn't mean you need a huge reward every time—but taking a moment to appreciate your efforts reinforces the positive changes you're making. Over time, these small wins accumulate, and your brain starts to recognize the value of positive behaviors and thoughts.

8. Stay Consistent

The key to rewiring your brain is consistency. Positive thinking isn't something that changes overnight—it's a habit that needs to be practiced daily. The more consistently you engage in activities that promote positivity—whether it's practicing gratitude, affirmations, mindfulness, or reframing negative thoughts—the more automatic those positive thoughts and behaviors will become.

Even on tough days, try to stay committed. Remember that consistency is more important than perfection. The more you show up for yourself, the easier it becomes to think positively, and over time, positivity will become your new default.

Conclusion

Rewiring your brain for positivity is a journey, not a destination. It requires effort, patience, and consistent practice. But the good news is that your brain is incredibly capable of change, and by taking small, intentional steps each day, you can gradually shift your mindset from negativity to positivity. As you practice gratitude, challenge your negative thoughts, use affirmations, and create a supportive environment, you'll find that positivity becomes more natural. With time and consistency, your brain will start to naturally gravitate toward positive thoughts, helping you create the life you truly desire.

Practical Step: Daily Mindset Rewiring Practices

Rewiring your mindset for success, happiness, and positivity doesn't happen overnight. It's a process that requires intentional daily effort. The good news is that small, consistent practices can have a profound impact on your brain and outlook on life. By incorporating simple yet powerful practices like gratitude and positive self-talk into your daily routine, you can gradually shift your mindset toward one that supports your growth, goals, and overall well-being.

Here are some practical, daily mindset rewiring practices that will help you create lasting change:

1. Start Your Day with Gratitude

Gratitude is one of the most powerful tools for rewiring your brain. When you start your day by focusing on what you're thankful for, you set a positive tone for the rest of your day. Gratitude shifts your focus from what's wrong in your life to what's going right. It trains your brain to look for abundance, rather than scarcity.

How to do it:

- When you wake up in the morning, take a few moments to list three things you are grateful for. These don't have to be grand—anything from a warm cup of coffee to your health or a kind gesture from a friend works. The goal is to start your day with an attitude of appreciation.

- You can also keep a gratitude journal. Each night, write down at least three things you were grateful for that day. Reflecting on the positive aspects of your life before bed can help you end your day on a peaceful and content note.

Why it works: Focusing on gratitude activates the brain's reward center, boosting dopamine and serotonin, which are associated with feelings of happiness and well-being. The more you practice gratitude, the more your brain will start looking for positive experiences in your life.

2. Positive Self-Talk and Affirmations

The way you speak to yourself shapes how you view yourself and the world. Negative self-talk keeps you stuck in limiting beliefs and self-doubt. On the other hand, positive self-talk and affirmations can help shift your thinking toward confidence and empowerment.

How to do it:

- Identify negative thoughts you frequently have about yourself. For example, if you often think, *"I'm not good enough,"* replace it with a positive affirmation like, *"I am capable, and I have the power to achieve my goals."*

- Write down a list of positive affirmations that resonate with you and reflect the person you want to become. For example:

  o *"I am worthy of success."*

  o *"I have everything I need to achieve my dreams."*

  o *"I am confident in my abilities."*

- Repeat these affirmations aloud or silently to yourself, ideally in the morning or before bed. The more you repeat them, the more your brain will begin to believe them.

Why it works: Affirmations work because they engage the brain's neuroplasticity, helping to rewire negative thought patterns and replace them with empowering ones. Repeating positive statements about yourself trains your brain to focus on your strengths rather than your weaknesses.

3. Mindfulness Meditation

Mindfulness is the practice of being present in the moment without judgment. Meditation, especially mindfulness meditation, helps you become aware of your thoughts and emotions and allows you to detach from negative patterns. This awareness creates space between your thoughts and your reactions, giving you more control over your mindset.

How to do it:

- Set aside 5-10 minutes each day to practice mindfulness meditation. Sit in a quiet space, close your eyes, and focus on your breath. When your mind wanders (and it will), gently bring your attention back to your breath without judgment.

- As you meditate, observe your thoughts without attachment. If a negative thought arises, don't engage with it—just notice it and let it pass.

- You can also use guided meditation apps that focus on gratitude, self-compassion, or positivity to help you stay centered.

Why it works: Mindfulness meditation trains your brain to focus on the present moment, reducing stress and anxiety. It helps you detach from negative thought patterns and develop a calmer, more positive perspective on life. Regular meditation has been shown to increase grey matter in areas of the brain related to emotional regulation, which supports a more balanced and positive mindset.

4. Reframe Negative Thoughts

Reframing is the practice of changing the way you perceive a situation, often turning a challenge into an opportunity. Reframing negative thoughts helps you break free from automatic, limiting beliefs and gives you the power to choose how you respond to life's obstacles.

How to do it:

- The next time you have a negative thought, pause and ask yourself: *"Is this thought serving me? What would be a more empowering way to view this situation?"*

- For example, if you think, *"I'm terrible at this,"* reframe it to something like, *"I'm still learning, and every mistake is an opportunity to grow."*

- Keep a list of positive reframes you can turn to when facing difficulties. Having a mental toolkit ready can help you navigate challenges with a positive mindset.

Why it works: Reframing helps you break free from fixed, negative thought patterns. It encourages your brain to look for solutions and opportunities, rather than dwelling on problems. By regularly practicing reframing, you'll train your brain to see the positive side of any situation.

5. Visualize Your Success

Visualization is a powerful practice that helps align your mind with your goals. When you visualize yourself succeeding, your brain starts to believe that success is possible, making it more likely that you will take action toward your dreams.

How to do it:

- Take a few minutes each day to close your eyes and vividly imagine yourself achieving your goals. See yourself living the life you desire—whether it's succeeding in your career, cultivating healthy relationships, or mastering a new skill.

- As you visualize, focus on the positive feelings associated with your success—pride, joy, excitement. The more sensory detail you can add to your visualization, the more powerful it will be.

Why it works: Visualization engages the same neural pathways that are activated when you actually perform an action. By mentally rehearsing success, you condition your brain to believe in the possibility of that success. This helps boost motivation, confidence, and a positive mindset.

6. Practice Self-Compassion

Rewiring your brain for positivity doesn't mean being hard on yourself when things don't go as planned. In fact, practicing self-compassion is essential for maintaining a positive mindset. Being kind to yourself helps you bounce back from setbacks and avoid falling into negative thinking spirals.

How to do it:

- When you make a mistake or face a challenge, practice speaking to yourself as you would to a friend. Instead of being self-critical, say things like, *"It's okay to make mistakes. I'm doing my best, and I'll learn from this."*

- Take care of your emotional well-being by setting boundaries, resting when needed, and treating yourself with love and kindness.

Why it works: Self-compassion allows you to acknowledge your flaws and mistakes without letting them define you. It helps you build resilience, reduce self-judgment, and maintain a positive, growth-oriented mindset.

Conclusion

Daily mindset rewiring practices, such as gratitude, positive self-talk, and mindfulness, are simple yet powerful tools that can help you shift your thinking from negativity to positivity. By making these practices a part of your daily routine, you begin to rewire your brain to automatically focus on the positive, empowering aspects of life. Over time, these small but consistent actions will transform your mindset, leading to a happier, more fulfilled life.

4

Replacing Doubt with Courage

The Root of Fear and Its Effect on Your Life

Fear is a primal emotion, hardwired into our brains to protect us from danger. It's a survival mechanism that triggers our "fight or flight" response when faced with threats, helping us stay alive. However, in modern life, most of our fears are not life-threatening. They often stem from imagined scenarios or the anticipation of failure, judgment, or loss. Understanding the root of fear and its impact on our lives is the first step in overcoming it.

The Origin of Fear: A Survival Mechanism Gone Awry

Fear originally evolved to protect us from physical harm. Our ancestors faced real dangers—wild animals, harsh environments, and the unpredictability of nature. Fear was the body's natural alarm system, prompting us to respond quickly and decisively. In today's world, while the physical dangers may be fewer, our brains still react to perceived threats in much the same way.

The problem is, many of our fears now are not about physical danger but emotional or psychological threats—fear of rejection, fear of failure, fear of change, or fear of the unknown. These fears may not have life-or-death consequences, but they can still feel overwhelming. Our brain can't always distinguish between real danger and perceived threats, which is why we often experience the same intense feelings of fear over situations that don't pose any actual harm.

Fear as a Limiting Force

When fear takes root, it can have a profound impact on our lives. Fear often holds us back from pursuing our dreams, taking risks, and living fully. It convinces us that we're not capable or worthy of success. The fear of failure, for example, can paralyze us and prevent us from trying new things. It creates an inner dialogue of doubt, telling us we're not good enough or that we'll never be able to handle the challenges ahead.

Fear can also lead to procrastination. When we're afraid of something—whether it's a big decision, a new job, or a difficult conversation—our natural tendency may be to avoid it altogether. We tell ourselves that we're not ready or that we'll deal with it later, but this only perpetuates the cycle of fear and inaction. The longer we avoid facing our fears, the more control they have over us.

The Impact of Fear on Our Well-Being

The effects of fear go beyond just missed opportunities or unfulfilled dreams. Fear can have a significant impact on our emotional and physical well-being. It can lead to chronic stress, anxiety, and feelings of inadequacy. The constant state of "fight or flight" that fear triggers keeps our bodies in a heightened state of tension, which over time can weaken our immune system, disrupt our sleep, and increase the risk of burnout.

Furthermore, fear can influence our relationships. When we're afraid of rejection or judgment, we may pull back from others, hide our true selves, or avoid being vulnerable. We might keep our feelings or ideas to ourselves because we fear they won't be accepted. As a result, fear can lead to isolation, loneliness, and a lack of connection with the people around us.

The Paradox of Fear: The Things We Fear Are Often Imagined

One of the most interesting aspects of fear is that it often involves scenarios that haven't even happened yet. We create worst-case scenarios in our minds, imagining the most negative outcome possible. We fear failure, but we may never even give ourselves the chance to succeed. The fear of judgment often keeps us from putting ourselves out there, even though the judgment we fear is rarely as harsh or real as we imagine.

The paradox of fear is that, most of the time, the things we fear are not as bad as we think they'll be. And often, the fear itself is the biggest obstacle standing between us and what we want to achieve. The longer we allow fear to control us, the bigger it grows in our minds, even if the reality is much less threatening.

How Fear Keeps Us Stuck

Fear doesn't just prevent us from taking action—it can also trap us in old patterns and habits. When we're afraid, we tend to cling to the familiar, even if it's not serving us. We avoid change because the unknown feels more dangerous than staying in our comfort zone. Fear can create a mental and emotional prison, where we stay stuck in situations, relationships, or jobs that no longer bring us joy or fulfilment.

Over time, this can lead to feelings of dissatisfaction and regret. We may look back and realize how much potential we allowed fear to keep hidden, how many opportunities we passed up, and how many dreams we left unfulfilled.

Recognizing Fear as a Signal, Not a Stopping Point

While fear can be limiting, it can also be a valuable signal. Fear often shows up when we're on the verge of growth, when we're about to step outside our comfort zone. Rather than seeing fear as something to avoid or eliminate, we can choose to see it as an indicator that we're on the right path. It's a sign that we are stretching ourselves, embracing new possibilities, and challenging ourselves to grow.

The key to overcoming fear is not to ignore it or push it away but to acknowledge it, understand its root cause, and take action in spite of it. By reframing fear as an opportunity for growth, we can begin to take back control and replace fear with courage.

The Transformative Power of Courage

When you choose to confront fear, you replace it with courage. Courage doesn't mean the absence of fear—it means feeling the fear and acting anyway. It means acknowledging the discomfort that comes with uncertainty and moving forward, even when the outcome is unclear. Courage is what allows us to take the first step toward our goals, even if we don't know exactly how it will unfold.

The more you practice courage, the easier it becomes to step into new opportunities and embrace the unknown. Over time, fear will lose its grip on your life, and you'll find yourself living more boldly, authentically, and freely.

In the end, fear doesn't have to control you. By understanding its roots and recognizing its effect on your life, you can begin to take proactive steps to overcome it. Replacing fear with courage will empower you to live with confidence, pursue your dreams, and step into the limitless potential within you.

How Fear Holds You Back from Limitless Thinking

Fear is one of the most powerful forces that can limit your potential and keep you from embracing a mindset of limitless possibilities. While fear is a natural and protective emotion, when it dominates your thoughts and actions, it becomes a barrier that prevents you from thinking big, taking risks, and pursuing your dreams. Fear, in its many forms, clouds your ability to see beyond your current circumstances and can trap you in a cycle of self-doubt and limitations.

Understanding how fear holds you back from limitless thinking is the first step in breaking free from its constraints. Once you recognize how fear operates in your life, you can begin to dismantle it, replacing it with courage, confidence, and the belief that you are capable of achieving anything.

1. Fear Keeps You in Your Comfort Zone

The primary way fear holds you back is by keeping you firmly rooted in your comfort zone. The comfort zone is where everything feels safe, predictable, and familiar. But the problem with staying in this zone is that it limits your growth and prevents you from exploring new opportunities. Fear whispers, *"Don't try that new thing; you might fail,"* or *"Stay where you are; this is enough."*

While your comfort zone might feel secure, it's also a place where limitless thinking can't flourish. The potential for innovation, creativity, and achievement lies outside of your comfort zone. When you're constantly afraid to step out, you never challenge your limits. As a result, you remain stagnant, unable to break free from the constraints you've placed on yourself.

2. Fear of Failure Paralyzes Your Action

One of the most common fears that hold people back from limitless thinking is the fear of failure. This fear convinces you that failure is something to be avoided at all costs, often leading to procrastination, indecision, or inaction altogether. When you're afraid to fail, you become overly cautious and hesitant, and instead of taking bold steps toward your goals, you stay in a state of uncertainty.

This fear of failure keeps you from seeing failure as a learning opportunity or a necessary part of growth. In reality, failure is often a stepping stone to success— it's a natural part of the journey that teaches you valuable lessons and helps refine your strategies. When you allow the fear of failure to dominate your thoughts, you shut down the possibility of growth and the opportunity to innovate and push boundaries.

3. Fear of Judgment Holds You Back from Authenticity

Fear of judgment—whether from others or from your own inner critic—is another major obstacle to limitless thinking. This fear makes you second-guess your ideas, opinions, and actions. You worry about what people will think, whether you'll be accepted, or if you'll be criticized for thinking or doing something different.

When you're afraid of judgment, you suppress your true self. You conform to what others expect of you and shy away from expressing your unique ideas. As a result, you limit your potential and miss out on opportunities to think creatively, take risks, and showcase your authentic self. True innovation and limitless thinking come from embracing your individuality, daring to think outside the box, and not worrying about others' opinions.

4. Fear of the Unknown Blocks New Opportunities

Another way fear holds you back from limitless thinking is by making the unknown seem like a daunting and dangerous place. The future is uncertain, and fear thrives on uncertainty. Fear makes you overestimate the dangers of venturing into unfamiliar territory, leading you to hold back from pursuing new ideas, relationships, or business ventures.

This fear of the unknown creates a mental block that prevents you from exploring new horizons. You become fixated on what could go wrong, rather than focusing on what could go right. Limitless thinking requires the ability to embrace uncertainty and step into the unknown with a sense of excitement rather than dread. Without this mindset, you're unlikely to take the necessary steps toward breakthroughs, growth, and success.

5. Fear of Success Creates Self-Sabotage

For some, the fear of success is just as limiting as the fear of failure. This might sound counterintuitive, but fear of success can stem from a deep belief that you don't deserve success, or that with success comes even greater responsibility and pressure. As a result, you might unconsciously self-sabotage, avoiding opportunities or engaging in behaviors that prevent you from achieving your goals.

When you're afraid of success, you limit your potential because you're not fully stepping into your power. You may downplay your achievements, settle for less, or avoid fully committing to your dreams. This fear keeps you from thinking big and seeing the vast potential you have within you. True limitless thinking involves believing that you are worthy of success and that your potential is unlimited.

6. Fear of Rejection Deters You from Connecting and Collaborating

Fear of rejection also plays a significant role in holding you back from limitless thinking, especially in social or professional contexts. This fear can make you hesitant to put yourself out there, whether it's by networking, sharing your ideas, or asking for help. The fear of being rejected by others can prevent you from building meaningful relationships, forming collaborations, or learning from others.

Limitless thinking thrives in an environment where ideas flow freely and where you're open to collaboration, feedback, and new perspectives. When you fear rejection, you miss out on the support, growth, and opportunities that come from connecting with others. You close yourself off from the very networks and resources that can help you expand your thinking and elevate your potential.

7. Fear of Not Being Good Enough Limits Your Self-Belief

At the core of many of our fears lies the belief that we're not good enough—that we lack the skills, talent, or resources to succeed. This fear of inadequacy directly affects your self-belief and self-worth, creating a barrier to limitless thinking. If you constantly feel like you're not enough, you'll hesitate to take bold steps or pursue ambitious goals. You'll limit your potential based on the belief that you're unqualified or undeserving of success.

The truth is, everyone experiences moments of doubt, but limitless thinking requires a mindset shift: from self-doubt to self-belief. It's about recognizing your unique strengths, embracing your potential, and trusting that you have what it takes to achieve your dreams. Fear of not being good enough only holds you back if you allow it to. Replacing it with the belief that you are capable opens the door to limitless possibilities.

Breaking Free from Fear to Embrace Limitless Thinking

To break free from the grip of fear and unlock limitless thinking, you must first acknowledge its presence in your life. Recognize the areas where fear holds you back—whether it's fear of failure, judgment, rejection, or the unknown—and begin to challenge it. Replace fear with courage, curiosity, and the willingness to step outside of your comfort zone.

As you confront fear, you'll find that your potential is far greater than you ever imagined. You'll start to see opportunities instead of obstacles and believe in the endless possibilities that lie before you. Limitless thinking isn't about being fearless; it's about moving forward in spite of fear, knowing that you have the power to create the life you desire.

Transforming Fear into Courage and Action

Fear is a natural part of the human experience. It's the emotional reaction that arises when we face the unknown, confront potential failure, or step outside of our comfort zones. But fear doesn't have to control us. In fact, it can be one of the most powerful catalysts for growth and transformation—if we learn how to transform it into courage and action.

When you understand that fear is not a signal to stop, but rather an invitation to rise to a new challenge, you can begin to shift your relationship with it. Fear can either paralyze you or propel you forward, depending on how you choose to respond. The key is to embrace it, use it as fuel, and take intentional steps toward action, even when it feels uncomfortable.

1. Acknowledge Fear Without Judgment

The first step in transforming fear is to acknowledge it without judgment. It's easy to fall into the trap of thinking that fear is something bad or that you should somehow be immune to it. But fear is simply a signal that you are moving into unfamiliar territory, which often means you're on the verge of growth.

Instead of suppressing or avoiding your fear, take a moment to recognize it. Say to yourself, *"I am feeling fear right now, and that's okay. It's a normal part of the process."* This acknowledgment allows you to take the power away from the fear, rather than letting it control you. The more you can accept fear as a part of your journey, the less it will hold you back.

2. Shift Your Focus: From Fear to Opportunity

Fear often arises from a focus on potential negative outcomes: *"What if I fail?"* or *"What if I'm not good enough?"* This perspective traps us in a cycle of worry and self-doubt, preventing us from taking action. To transform fear into courage, you must consciously shift your focus from the potential for failure to the opportunity for growth.

Start by reframing your fear into something positive. Instead of thinking, *"What if I fail?"* ask yourself, *"What can I learn from this? How can I grow through this experience?"* This simple shift in perspective turns fear into a powerful motivator for growth. It encourages you to see challenges not as threats but as opportunities to develop new skills, gain valuable insights, and push beyond your current limits.

3. Take Small, Purposeful Steps Toward Action

Fear often paralyzes us because the task at hand feels too big or overwhelming. The key to transforming fear into action is to break down the challenge into smaller, more manageable steps. Each small action you take helps build momentum and reduces the intensity of the fear.

If you're afraid of starting something new—whether it's launching a business, having a difficult conversation, or pursuing a big goal—take one small step toward it. It doesn't have to be a giant leap. Just start somewhere. Maybe it's researching, making a phone call, or even just writing down your thoughts. These initial steps, though small, create movement and break the inertia that fear creates.

By focusing on progress rather than perfection, you allow yourself to take consistent action, which gradually reduces the power that fear has over you.

4. Use the Power of Visualization to Build Confidence

Visualization is a powerful tool in transforming fear into courage. When you visualize yourself succeeding—whether it's landing a big project, speaking confidently in front of an audience, or overcoming a personal challenge—you prime your brain for success. Visualization helps shift your mindset from one of fear to one of belief.

Before taking any action that evokes fear, close your eyes and imagine yourself succeeding. Picture every detail of the process: how you'll feel, what success will look like, and how you'll handle obstacles along the way. The more vivid and detailed your visualization, the more real and achievable your success will seem.

This technique not only boosts confidence but also helps you feel more capable and prepared, reducing the fear that often holds you back from taking the first step.

5. Reframe Fear as Fuel for Growth

Fear has a lot of energy to offer. The rush of adrenaline and the heightened sense of alertness that come with fear are the body's way of preparing for action. Instead of viewing fear as something to avoid, you can transform it into a source of energy that fuels your progress.

Next time fear arises, instead of backing away, lean into it. Feel the fear and acknowledge that it's a signal that you are pushing yourself beyond your limits. Recognize that fear is an indication that you're growing, that you're on the verge of something important. Channel the energy of fear into motivation to take action, knowing that this discomfort is often the precursor to something extraordinary.

6. Practice Self-Compassion and Patience

Fear often brings with it a sense of urgency or a fear of making mistakes. You may feel as though you need to have everything figured out or that you need to act perfectly from the start. However, perfectionism can feed into fear, making it even harder to take action.

Instead of expecting perfection, practice self-compassion. Be kind to yourself when fear arises and remind yourself that you are doing your best. Acknowledge that fear is a part of the process and that you will learn along the way. The more patient and forgiving you are with yourself, the less likely you are to be paralyzed by fear.

Self-compassion helps reduce the pressure you place on yourself, making it easier to take imperfect but meaningful action. This mindset shift helps transform fear into courage by allowing you to move forward despite the inevitable setbacks and challenges.

7. Celebrate Every Step Forward

As you begin to take action, no matter how small, celebrate your progress. Every step you take toward overcoming fear is a victory. By acknowledging and celebrating these moments, you reinforce the idea that action, even in the face of fear, is worth it. This positive reinforcement helps create a feedback loop, where the more action you take, the more confidence you build, and the less power fear has over you.

Celebrate your courage, your resilience, and your willingness to step into the unknown. The more you embrace these small wins, the more you'll be empowered to keep pushing forward, transforming fear into a constant source of motivation and action.

Conclusion: Courage is Not the Absence of Fear

Fear will always be a part of the journey, but it doesn't have to control your life or your decisions. By acknowledging fear, shifting your focus to opportunity, taking small actions, visualizing success, and practicing self-compassion, you can transform fear into courage and action.

Remember, courage isn't about being fearless—it's about feeling the fear and choosing to move forward anyway. Each time you take action in the face of fear, you reinforce your ability to act with courage and confidence. Over time, these small acts of bravery accumulate and propel you toward limitless possibilities. Fear may never completely disappear, but you can choose to rise above it, using it as a powerful tool to drive you toward the life you deserve.

Visualizing Your Success and Facing Your Fears Head-On

Visualization is one of the most powerful tools in creating the life you want. It taps into the brain's ability to perceive the future as if it's happening in the present moment. By using this technique, you're not only seeing your success before it happens but also conditioning your mind to believe in the possibility of achieving it. But even more than that, visualization can help you face your fears head-on, transforming the anxiety and uncertainty that often hold you back into a clear path forward.

1. The Power of Visualization: Seeing Success Before It Happens

Visualization is more than daydreaming about your dreams—it's an intentional mental exercise that shapes the reality you want to create. When you visualize success, you're wiring your brain for positive outcomes. Studies have shown that the brain doesn't differentiate much between something vividly imagined and something physically experienced. This means that when you mentally rehearse success—whether it's acing a presentation, landing a job, or overcoming a personal challenge—your brain believes it's already happened, boosting your confidence and preparing you for the real thing.

By consistently visualizing yourself succeeding, you begin to see possibilities where you once saw obstacles. You become more resilient because your mind already "knows" how to navigate challenges and how to feel when you accomplish your goal. Success becomes less about chance and more about inevitability, because your brain is wired to find the ways to make it happen.

2. Embracing Fear as Part of the Process

Fear is often one of the most significant roadblocks to reaching our potential. It's a natural response to stepping into the unknown, and yet, too often, we let it paralyze us. What we forget, however, is that fear is not something to avoid or be ashamed of—it's simply a part of the process. Every time you challenge yourself to do something new, fear will show up, but it doesn't have to stop you.

Visualization is incredibly helpful in this process because it allows you to mentally rehearse not only your success but also the challenges and fears that may arise along the way. Rather than letting fear catch you off guard, you can use your mind to prepare for it.

Picture yourself in the situation that scares you—whether it's giving a speech, taking a leap in your career, or having a tough conversation. See the fear, but also see yourself overcoming it. Imagine how you'll feel when you push through the discomfort and keep moving forward. This exercise primes you to face your fears head-on when they appear, making it easier to navigate them with grace and confidence.

3. Breaking Down the Fear: Why It's Not as Scary as It Seems

When we're afraid of something, we often make it seem bigger and more intimidating than it truly is. Our minds tend to focus on worst-case scenarios, amplifying the fear to the point where we feel completely overwhelmed. Visualization can help counter this by allowing you to break down the fear into manageable, less intimidating parts.

For instance, instead of visualizing yourself failing in front of an audience, break it down. Picture yourself walking onto the stage, feeling the slight nerves in your stomach, but also imagining yourself breathing deeply and finding your rhythm. See yourself delivering your message with clarity, no matter how small the hiccups might be along the way. As you practice visualizing these steps, you'll begin to realize that the fear of the unknown isn't as intense as your mind initially made it out to be.

This process of breaking down your fears, through visualization, allows you to desensitize yourself to them, making them less daunting and ultimately less powerful.

4. Transforming Fear into a Source of Motivation

Instead of viewing fear as a force that holds you back, you can choose to see it as an energy source that propels you forward. Fear is simply a signal that you're stepping into uncharted territory, and that's when true growth occurs.

When you visualize your success, acknowledge the fear in your mind, and then consciously choose to use that fear as fuel. For example, imagine your fear as a physical force—perhaps it feels like a tight knot in your stomach or a racing heart. Rather than resisting it, envision that energy moving through your body, propelling you into action. As you push past that initial discomfort, you become more powerful and confident. The more you visualize your success in this way—using fear as a catalyst for action—the easier it becomes to confront and conquer it in real life.

5. Visualizing Your Success in the Face of Adversity

One of the most effective ways to use visualization in overcoming fear is to not just imagine success, but also visualize yourself navigating challenges and setbacks. In reality, there will always be obstacles, but it's how you respond to them that determines your success. By mentally rehearsing how you'll handle adversity—whether it's making a mistake, facing criticism, or dealing with unexpected delays—you prepare yourself to stay calm and resilient when things don't go as planned.

For instance, you might visualize yourself facing a difficult situation at work. Maybe you're presenting an idea to a team and they don't immediately respond the way you hoped. Instead of freezing up, you see yourself taking a deep breath, listening to their feedback, and adjusting your approach calmly and confidently. In this way, you're preparing yourself for the reality that fear will not only show up but that you have the strength and resilience to handle it.

6. The Mind-Body Connection: Acting as If You've Already Achieved Your Goal

Visualization works best when you pair it with physical actions that align with your imagined success. The mind-body connection is incredibly powerful—when you visualize your success, embody it physically by acting as if you've already achieved your goal. If you're preparing for a big presentation, stand tall, take deep breaths, and speak with the same confidence you envision. If you're afraid of rejection in a relationship, act with openness and vulnerability, as though you already have the love and acceptance you desire.

When you align your actions with your visualized success, you begin to rewire your brain to recognize success as your new normal. Over time, this creates a positive feedback loop where the fear starts to fade, and your confidence grows stronger.

7. Visualize the Bigger Picture: What's on the Other Side of Fear?

When you're in the midst of fear, it can be easy to get caught up in the discomfort of the moment. However, visualization allows you to zoom out and see the bigger picture. What lies beyond the fear? What is the bigger vision that you're moving toward?

Imagine the life you'll have once you break through your fears—the freedom, the opportunities, the personal growth. See yourself on the other side of fear, stronger, more confident, and proud of how you faced the challenges head-on. Visualizing this future helps you move past the temporary discomfort and refocus on the incredible rewards that await you once you take action.

Conclusion: Embracing Fear as the Gateway to Your Success

Visualizing your success and facing your fears head-on is a transformative process that allows you to move beyond your limitations and unlock your fullest potential. Fear is not something to avoid—it's a signal that you're on the verge of something great. By practicing visualization, you train your mind to see possibilities instead of barriers, to turn fear into motivation, and to embrace challenges as opportunities for growth.

As you continue to visualize your success and take action despite your fears, you'll find that what once seemed daunting becomes easier to handle. Fear no longer has the power to stop you—instead, it becomes the fuel that propels you toward a limitless future.

Practical Step: Create a Fear Confrontation Action Plan

Fear has the power to keep us stuck, to paralyze us from taking action, and to hold us back from reaching our fullest potential. But what if you could use that fear as a catalyst for growth? What if you could face your fears head-on and take purposeful steps toward overcoming them? Creating a Fear Confrontation Action Plan is a practical tool that empowers you to tackle your fears with intention, structure, and a clear strategy.

This plan will help you move from feeling overwhelmed by fear to feeling confident and capable of taking the necessary actions to break through it. It's not about eliminating fear entirely, but rather learning how to face it with courage and turn it into a powerful motivator for change.

Step 1: Identify Your Fear

The first step in creating your Fear Confrontation Action Plan is to clearly identify the fear you want to overcome. Fear can sometimes be vague or abstract, so it's important to bring it into focus. What are you afraid of? Is it fear of failure, rejection, criticism, the unknown, or perhaps fear of success?

Be specific about what triggers your fear. Is it speaking in public, starting a new business, or asking for a promotion at work? The more precise you can be in identifying your fear, the easier it will be to address it effectively. Write it down. Getting it out of your head and onto paper helps create clarity.

Example: *I fear speaking in front of large groups because I'm afraid I'll forget my words or be judged by others.*

Step 2: Break It Down

Once you've identified your fear, break it down into smaller, more manageable pieces. Often, fear feels overwhelming because we see it as a large, insurmountable obstacle. By breaking it down, you can see the individual steps that will lead to overcoming it.

Ask yourself: What is the root of this fear? What exactly am I afraid will happen? For example, in the case of public speaking, you might fear forgetting your lines or not making a good impression. These are more specific fears that you can address one by one.

Example: *My fear of public speaking breaks down into three parts: 1) Forgetting my lines, 2) Looking nervous and unprepared, 3) Being judged by the audience.*

Step 3: Visualize Success and Prepare for Challenges

Visualization is a powerful tool for overcoming fear. It trains your brain to see the successful outcome rather than the worst-case scenario. Take a few moments to close your eyes and visualize yourself successfully confronting your fear.

Imagine yourself in the situation where you feel afraid. Picture yourself acting with confidence, handling challenges gracefully, and succeeding. This not only prepares your mind for success but also helps desensitize you to the fear by normalizing the experience in your mind.

But visualization isn't just about seeing success—it's also about mentally preparing for challenges. What could go wrong? How will you handle it? Anticipating obstacles and planning for them can help you stay calm and collected when things don't go perfectly.

Example: *I visualize myself walking up to the podium, feeling the nerves, but confidently speaking and making a strong connection with my audience. If I forget a word, I see myself pausing, taking a deep breath, and continuing without missing a beat.*

Step 4: Set Realistic Goals and Action Steps

The next step is to break your fear down into actionable steps. Rather than focusing on the fear itself, focus on small, manageable actions that will help you gradually face and conquer it. Setting realistic goals is key to making progress and building confidence.

Start with small, low-stakes actions that will help you build momentum. For example, if you're afraid of public speaking, you might begin by practicing in front of a mirror, then progress to speaking in front of a friend or family member, and eventually move on to larger audiences. Each step will bring you closer to conquering the fear.

Example: *I will start by practicing my speech in front of a mirror for 10 minutes each day. Then, I'll record myself to see where I can improve. Afterward, I'll practice in front of a trusted friend and ask for feedback. Finally, I'll schedule my first small speaking opportunity.*

Step 5: Reframe Negative Thoughts and Self-Talk

One of the most powerful ways to confront your fear is to shift your mindset. Often, fear is fueled by negative self-talk—thoughts like *"I'm not good enough"* or *"I'm going to fail."* These thoughts only feed into your fear, making it stronger.

Reframing your negative thoughts into more empowering and supportive statements can help you replace fear with confidence. Challenge your limiting beliefs by asking yourself: *Is this thought really true? What evidence do I have that contradicts it? What positive affirmation can I use instead?*

For example, instead of thinking *"I'm going to fail,"* reframe it as *"I am capable of doing my best, and I will learn and grow from any mistakes I make."* By consistently practicing positive self-talk, you'll weaken the grip of fear on your mind.

Example: *Instead of thinking, "I'll forget everything and embarrass myself," I will reframe it as "I've prepared, I know my material, and I have the ability to handle any situation that comes my way."*

Step 6: Take Action—One Step at a Time

The most important step in your Fear Confrontation Action Plan is to take action. Fear thrives in a state of inaction; the longer you wait, the bigger it becomes in your mind. Taking action, even if it's small, is the key to breaking the cycle of fear.

Start with the smallest, least intimidating action in your plan. This could be as simple as writing your speech, sending an email, or signing up for a course. Each small step you take will help build your confidence and weaken the hold that fear has over you. With each action, you'll also reinforce your belief that you can handle the discomfort of fear.

Example: *Today, I will spend 10 minutes writing out the introduction to my speech. Tomorrow, I'll practice saying it aloud in front of the mirror. These small steps will help me prepare for the bigger moments ahead.*

Step 7: Celebrate Your Progress

Finally, make sure to celebrate each small victory along the way. Overcoming fear is a process, and it's important to recognize your growth and progress. Each time you confront your fear, you're becoming stronger, more resilient, and more capable of achieving your goals.

Acknowledge your accomplishments, no matter how small they may seem. This helps build positive momentum and reinforces the belief that you are capable of overcoming fear.

Example: *After practicing my speech in front of a friend, I will celebrate by treating myself to something I enjoy, like a coffee or a walk in the park.*

Conclusion: Moving Beyond Fear to Embrace Action

Creating a Fear Confrontation Action Plan is a powerful way to take control of your fears, rather than allowing them to control you. By identifying your fear, breaking it down into manageable steps, visualizing success, reframing your negative thoughts, and taking consistent action, you can slowly transform fear from an obstacle into a source of motivation.

Remember, the goal is not to eliminate fear completely—it's about learning how to face it, take action in spite of it, and continue moving forward toward the life you desire. Fear is not a signal to stop; it's an invitation to grow. With your action plan in hand, you're ready to embrace the discomfort and turn it into the courage and strength needed to transform your life.

5

From Self-Doubt to Unshakable Confidence

Identifying the Core of Low Self-Esteem

Self-esteem, at its core, is the way we perceive and value ourselves. It's the lens through which we view our abilities, our worth, and our place in the world. When self-esteem is high, we feel capable, confident, and deserving of success. However, when it's low, we often struggle with feelings of inadequacy, self-doubt, and the belief that we're not enough.

Understanding the root causes of low self-esteem is the first step toward building unshakable confidence. Low self-esteem doesn't develop overnight; it's often the result of a combination of past experiences, negative self-talk, and societal influences. To transform it, we must first identify what's feeding it. Only by understanding its origins can we start the process of healing and growth.

1. Childhood Experiences and Conditioning

For many, the foundation of low self-esteem is built in childhood. The messages we receive from parents, teachers, peers, and society during our formative years play a critical role in shaping our self-image. If we grow up in an environment where we're criticized, neglected, or not shown enough love and affirmation, we may internalize the belief that we're not worthy of love or success.

On the other hand, even well-meaning praise can sometimes create unrealistic expectations, leading to a constant need for validation. If you were often praised for achievements or appearance rather than for intrinsic qualities like kindness, intelligence, or effort, you might come to believe that your worth is tied solely to performance or how others perceive you. This can set the stage for a fragile sense of self-esteem that is easily shaken by criticism or failure.

Reflection Exercise: Think back to your childhood—what messages did you receive about yourself? How did your caregivers or significant figures in your life make you feel about your abilities or worth? Write down any experiences that may have shaped your sense of self.

2. Negative Self-Talk and Limiting Beliefs

Another core factor in low self-esteem is the constant stream of negative self-talk. The voice inside our heads often becomes our worst enemy, filling our thoughts with self-criticism, doubt, and judgment. *"I'm not good enough," "I'll never succeed,"* or *"I'm a failure"* are common thoughts that feed feelings of inadequacy.

These thoughts don't just reflect our current state—they shape it. Repeating negative beliefs about ourselves leads to a self-fulfilling prophecy. If you constantly tell yourself you're not capable or deserving of success, you'll start avoiding opportunities that challenge those beliefs, which only reinforces the cycle of low self-esteem.

Limiting beliefs are another aspect of negative self-talk. These are deep-seated convictions that limit our potential, such as believing *"I'm not smart enough"* or *"I don't deserve love."* These beliefs often stem from past experiences and can become so ingrained in our psyche that we start to live in accordance with them, rather than challenging them.

Reflection Exercise: Start paying attention to your self-talk. Write down the negative thoughts you have about yourself throughout the day. Do they align with limiting beliefs? Challenge these thoughts by asking yourself: *Are they based on facts, or are they assumptions or past experiences that no longer define me?*

3. Comparing Yourself to Others

In today's world of social media and constant connectivity, it's easy to fall into the trap of comparing ourselves to others. Whether it's their appearance, achievements, relationships, or lifestyle, we can easily feel like we don't measure up. Social comparison is a major contributor to feelings of inadequacy and low self-worth.

What we often forget is that comparison is inherently unfair. We are comparing our behind-the-scenes struggles to other people's highlight reels. No one's life is as perfect as it appears online, but when we place our self-worth on these comparisons, we set ourselves up for disappointment and self-doubt.

Constantly comparing yourself to others can lead to feelings of envy, frustration, and a belief that you're not doing enough or being enough. This erodes your sense of self-worth because you begin to tie your value to external standards, rather than your own intrinsic qualities and capabilities.

Reflection Exercise: Think about the last time you compared yourself to someone else. What emotions did it stir up? How did it make you feel about yourself? Recognize that your self-worth should never be based on someone else's life or accomplishments.

4. Fear of Judgment and Rejection

Fear of judgment and rejection is a powerful driver of low self-esteem. It's human nature to want to be accepted and validated by others. However, when we constantly fear judgment or rejection, it can prevent us from fully expressing ourselves or taking risks. This fear can become so ingrained that it leads us to hold back from pursuing our goals, speaking our truth, or even engaging with others authentically.

When we fear rejection, we tend to put up walls to protect ourselves. We might avoid situations where we feel vulnerable, stay in the background, or silence our opinions. Over time, this avoidance behavior chips away at our confidence, reinforcing the belief that we're not worthy of acceptance or success.

The truth is, rejection and judgment are a part of life, and they don't define our worth. Every successful person has faced rejection or criticism, and they've learned to use those experiences as stepping stones to growth.

Reflection Exercise: Are there areas of your life where you're holding back because of fear of judgment? Write about a time when you were rejected or judged and reflect on how it made you feel. How can you reframe that experience in a way that empowers you?

5. Past Failures and Setbacks

Our failures, especially those that occur in significant moments, can leave a deep imprint on our self-esteem. When we fail at something—whether it's a personal goal, a project at work, or a relationship—it's easy to internalize that failure and believe that it reflects our worth as a person. We begin to equate our failures with our identity, thinking *"I failed, so I am a failure."*

This kind of thinking is detrimental because it doesn't account for the lessons and growth that come from failure. Failure is not the opposite of success; it's a part of it. Every great achievement comes with moments of misstep and learning. To break free from low self-esteem, we must reframe our past failures as valuable learning experiences rather than reflections of our value.

Reflection Exercise: Think about a failure or setback you've experienced. Instead of seeing it as a reflection of your worth, how can you view it as a lesson or stepping stone to success? What did it teach you about yourself and your resilience?

6. Perfectionism

Perfectionism is another root cause of low self-esteem. When we set impossibly high standards for ourselves, we are constantly setting ourselves up for failure. Perfectionism creates an inner narrative of *"I'm not good enough unless I am perfect."* This can prevent us from taking action, as we fear not meeting the mark. As a result, we may avoid trying altogether or constantly feel dissatisfied with our efforts, no matter how much we accomplish.

Perfectionism also ties our worth to our ability to perform flawlessly, making it impossible to feel truly good about ourselves. Learning to embrace imperfection and accept that mistakes are part of being human is essential to building self-esteem.

Reflection Exercise: Are you a perfectionist? How does it affect your self-esteem? Write about an instance when perfectionism stopped you from taking action, and how embracing imperfection could have changed the outcome.

Conclusion: Moving Forward with Awareness

Identifying the core of low self-esteem is an essential first step in building lasting confidence. Once you understand the root causes—whether from childhood experiences, negative self-talk, societal pressures, or past failures—you can begin to challenge the beliefs and patterns that have kept you stuck.

Remember, low self-esteem is not a permanent state. It's something that can be changed with conscious effort, self-awareness, and a commitment to reshaping the way you view yourself. By recognizing the sources of self-doubt, you gain the power to change your narrative and begin the journey toward unshakable confidence.

Why Believing in Yourself is the First Step to Transformation

---

Transformation begins within. It starts with a simple yet profound truth: **you are capable**. The belief in yourself is the most powerful catalyst for change. Without it, no external circumstances—no matter how favorable—can truly lead to lasting transformation. Self-belief isn't about being arrogant or thinking you're invincible; it's about trusting your potential and having the courage to pursue the life you envision, regardless of the challenges.

When you believe in yourself, you shift from a mindset of limitation to one of possibility. You begin to see the world not as a place where you are powerless but as a canvas where you can create, shape, and change your reality. This belief sets the foundation for everything else in your life—your actions, your decisions, and ultimately, your results.

1. Self-Belief Fuels Motivation and Action

Transformation requires action. And to take bold, transformative actions, you need the fuel of self-belief. When you believe in yourself, you are more likely to take risks, step out of your comfort zone, and pursue opportunities that align with your goals. This confidence helps you push past fear and self-doubt, even when the road ahead seems uncertain.

Without self-belief, fear of failure or judgment can paralyze you. You might hesitate to take the first step because you don't trust your abilities or worth. But when you believe that you have the strength and capability to navigate the challenges ahead, you are motivated to take action. You'll move forward with a sense of purpose, knowing that even if you stumble along the way, you have what it takes to rise again.

Example: Think about a time when you felt confident about a decision you made or a goal you set. That belief likely gave you the energy to take the necessary steps, even if things were difficult. That's the power of self-belief.

2. Belief Opens the Door to New Possibilities

When you believe in yourself, you open your mind to new possibilities. If you're stuck in a cycle of self-doubt, you're limiting the opportunities you'll even consider. But when you trust in your abilities, you begin to see a world full of potential. Instead of saying "I can't," you'll find yourself asking "How can I?" You shift from a mindset of scarcity to one of abundance—there is always a way forward.

Believing in yourself allows you to recognize opportunities that may have seemed impossible before. It encourages you to think creatively and find solutions to obstacles. With this mindset, you stop seeing challenges as roadblocks and start viewing them as stepping stones to growth. You begin to realize that **every setback is an opportunity for a comeback**, every failure a lesson on the way to success.

Example: Imagine wanting to change careers but feeling stuck in your current job. Without self-belief, you might assume you don't have the right skills or that it's too late for a change. But when you believe in yourself, you're more likely to research new opportunities, gain new skills, and ultimately make the leap into something more fulfilling.

3. Belief Inspires Resilience and Perseverance

No journey of transformation is without obstacles. The path to change is often paved with setbacks, challenges, and moments of doubt. But self-belief gives you the resilience to keep going, even when the going gets tough. When you believe in your own strength, you understand that temporary failures do not define you.

People who trust in their abilities bounce back from setbacks more easily. They don't let adversity defeat them; instead, they view difficulties as part of the process. When you believe in yourself, you develop a "never give up" mentality. You understand that progress is rarely linear, but that doesn't stop you from moving forward. Each time you face an obstacle, you see it as an opportunity to grow stronger, wiser, and more capable.

Example: Consider someone training for a marathon. If they don't believe in their ability to finish, the first signs of fatigue or injury might make them quit. But if they truly believe they can achieve their goal, they will push through the pain, trusting that they have the inner strength to persevere and cross the finish line.

4. Self-Belief Transforms Your Mindset

The way you view yourself shapes your experience of the world. If you see yourself as incapable or unworthy, your actions will reflect that mindset. You might shy away from opportunities or believe that success is for others, not for you. On the other hand, when you believe in yourself, your mindset becomes one of possibility, empowerment, and hope.

A positive self-belief shifts your internal narrative. Instead of focusing on your perceived weaknesses, you start recognizing your strengths. You stop asking, "What if I fail?" and start asking, "What if I succeed?" This shift in perspective is the key to transformation. It enables you to approach life's challenges with a sense of excitement rather than fear.

Example: Think about someone starting a new business. At first, they might feel overwhelmed by the challenges, but their belief in themselves allows them to stay focused on their goals, adapt to changes, and stay persistent when things don't go as planned.

5. Belief Attracts Positive Energy and People

When you believe in yourself, you project an energy that is magnetic. People are drawn to those who are confident, authentic, and self-assured. This doesn't mean you have to have all the answers, but it means you trust yourself enough to take action and learn along the way. This self-assurance encourages others to believe in you, too.

In many cases, believing in yourself is the first step toward building relationships, partnerships, and networks that support your growth. You begin to attract people who uplift you, challenge you, and support your vision for transformation. Your belief in yourself creates a ripple effect that extends beyond you—it creates a world of possibility and connection.

Example: Think about the difference between someone who walks into a room with confidence and someone who is unsure of themselves. The confident person is likely to make connections more easily, to gain the support they need, and to inspire others around them. Confidence is magnetic, and believing in yourself is the first step in cultivating that energy.

6. Belief in Yourself Builds a Strong Foundation for Success

At the core of every successful person's journey is a deep, unwavering belief in themselves. They may not have had all the resources, the perfect circumstances, or the easiest path, but their belief in their ability to succeed gave them the foundation they needed to keep going. Believing in yourself is the bedrock on which all other success is built.

When you believe in yourself, you naturally take steps to build the life you desire. You invest in your growth, pursue opportunities with passion, and face challenges with a mindset of determination. Success becomes less about achieving external validation and more about aligning with your purpose and potential.

Example: Think about entrepreneurs who start with little more than an idea and a belief in themselves. They often face rejection, financial strain, and countless obstacles, but their belief keeps them moving forward. In the end, it's not the lack of resources that determines their success; it's the strength of their self-belief and their commitment to making their vision a reality.

Conclusion: Embrace the Power of Self-Belief

Believing in yourself is the starting point for any transformation. Without self-belief, no amount of external success or validation will be enough to make you feel truly fulfilled. But when you trust your potential, you unlock the power to overcome obstacles, create new opportunities, and build a life that aligns with your dreams.

Transformation begins from within, and it starts with the simple yet powerful decision to believe in yourself. You are capable. You are worthy. And with this belief, you can achieve anything you set your mind to. The journey toward the best version of yourself begins the moment you choose to believe that you are already enough.

Cultivating a Mindset of Self-Compassion and Respect

In the journey toward transformation and self-growth, one of the most important shifts you can make is adopting a mindset of self-compassion and respect. Too often, we are our own harshest critics, constantly focusing on our flaws, mistakes, and imperfections. We demand perfection from ourselves, and when we fall short, we respond with judgment and guilt. But self-compassion isn't about excusing our shortcomings; it's about acknowledging our humanity and treating ourselves with the same kindness, understanding, and respect that we would offer to a close friend.

Cultivating a mindset of self-compassion and respect doesn't mean we stop striving for growth or improvement. On the contrary, it creates a foundation of emotional resilience and inner peace that allows us to pursue our goals with grace and patience. It means recognizing that we are worthy of love and respect, not because we're perfect, but because we are human. And as humans, we are inherently deserving of compassion—especially from ourselves.

1. Understanding Self-Compassion

Self-compassion is the practice of treating yourself with kindness and care during moments of struggle, failure, or pain. It's about embracing your imperfections rather than criticizing them. When you practice self-compassion, you acknowledge your feelings without judgment and allow yourself to be vulnerable and imperfect without feeling ashamed.

Instead of responding to your mistakes with harsh criticism, self-compassion allows you to view them as opportunities for learning and growth. Instead of thinking, *"I failed, and that means I'm a failure,"* you learn to say, *"I made a mistake, and that's okay. It's part of the process of becoming better."*

A self-compassionate mindset acknowledges that suffering, failure, and mistakes are a universal part of the human experience. You're not alone in feeling challenged or discouraged. In fact, showing yourself compassion is often what gives you the strength to keep going, even when things don't go according to plan.

Example: Think of a time when you made a mistake—perhaps at work, in a relationship, or in pursuing a personal goal. How did you respond to that mistake? Were you critical and unforgiving, or did you offer yourself kindness and understanding? The next time you slip up, remind yourself that mistakes are part of being human and give yourself the grace to learn from them without judgment.

2. The Importance of Self-Respect

Self-respect goes hand in hand with self-compassion. It involves honoring your values, boundaries, and needs. It means treating yourself with the same regard and dignity that you would offer to others. When you have self-respect, you do not settle for less than you deserve. You value your time, energy, and emotional well-being, and you don't let others treat you in ways that compromise your worth.

Self-respect also involves making choices that align with your authentic self. It's about saying no to things that drain you, standing up for yourself in difficult situations, and prioritizing your own happiness and health. When you respect yourself, you create a life that reflects your values, and you stop allowing external influences to dictate your worth.

In many ways, self-respect is the foundation for healthy relationships—both with others and with yourself. You teach others how to treat you by first showing respect for yourself. And as you cultivate self-respect, you start to create a life that honors your needs, desires, and potential.

Example: Think about a situation where you allowed someone to overstep your boundaries or take advantage of your time and energy. How did that make you feel? When you respect yourself, you recognize when your boundaries are being violated and take steps to assert them, knowing that doing so is a reflection of your value and worth.

3. The Power of Self-Compassion in Overcoming Challenges

Life is full of challenges, obstacles, and unexpected setbacks. When you encounter these difficulties, it's easy to become discouraged or defeated, particularly if you don't practice self-compassion. Instead of seeing challenges as temporary hurdles, you might see them as proof of your inadequacy. This mindset can lead to frustration, anxiety, and even self-sabotage.

Self-compassion changes this narrative. It allows you to face challenges with a sense of calm and patience. Instead of responding to setbacks with criticism or frustration, you approach them with a mindset of curiosity and kindness. You recognize that it's normal to struggle, and that these struggles are not an indication of failure, but a part of the process of personal growth.

When you embrace self-compassion, you also learn to forgive yourself when things go wrong. You stop holding onto guilt and shame, which only weigh you down and keep you stuck in the past. Instead, you focus on moving forward with the knowledge that mistakes don't define you—they refine you.

Example: Imagine you're facing a tough project or goal, and you hit a roadblock. Without self-compassion, you might start to berate yourself for not being "good enough" or "smart enough." But with self-compassion, you would acknowledge the difficulty of the situation, be kind to yourself for feeling frustrated, and then refocus on finding a solution. This mindset shift allows you to stay resilient in the face of obstacles.

4. Practicing Self-Compassion Through Positive Self-Talk

Our internal dialogue plays a huge role in how we feel about ourselves. If we're constantly engaging in negative self-talk, we reinforce feelings of inadequacy, fear, and self-doubt. On the other hand, practicing self-compassion involves changing that inner dialogue. It's about replacing critical thoughts with nurturing, encouraging words.

Instead of saying, *"I'm not good enough,"* you might say, *"I'm doing the best I can, and that's enough."* Instead of thinking, *"I'll never succeed,"* you might remind yourself, *"Every step I take is progress, and I'm capable of overcoming challenges."*

This shift in self-talk helps to build self-worth and confidence. It encourages a mindset that is grounded in acceptance rather than perfection, and it helps you navigate difficult times with more grace and less stress.

Example: The next time you make a mistake or experience a setback, pay attention to your thoughts. Are they kind or critical? Try replacing any negative self-talk with compassionate statements like, *"It's okay to not be perfect, I'm still learning and growing."* This simple practice can have a profound impact on how you feel about yourself.

5. Building a Habit of Self-Care

Self-compassion isn't just about how you think about yourself—it's also about how you treat yourself. Practicing self-care is a key aspect of cultivating self-compassion and respect. Taking care of your physical, emotional, and mental health shows yourself that you are worthy of time and attention.

Self-care can take many forms, from getting enough rest to setting aside time for activities that nourish your soul. It can involve seeking support from others, saying no to things that drain you, or simply taking a few moments each day to be present and mindful. The key is to recognize that you deserve to care for yourself, and by doing so, you're honoring your needs and well-being.

Example: Reflect on your self-care practices. Do you make time for rest, relaxation, and activities that bring you joy? If not, start small. Prioritize your well-being, whether it's through a walk in nature, a warm bath, or time spent with loved ones. These moments of care reinforce your value and encourage you to continue showing up for yourself.

Conclusion: Embracing Self-Compassion and Respect

Cultivating a mindset of self-compassion and respect is not a one-time practice—it's a lifelong commitment to treating yourself with kindness, care, and honor. When you embrace self-compassion, you create a foundation of emotional strength that allows you to face life's challenges with resilience and grace. You recognize that you are worthy of love, care, and respect, no matter what imperfections you may have.

By practicing self-compassion and self-respect, you not only improve your relationship with yourself, but you also become more capable of creating the life you desire. It's from this place of love and understanding that true transformation can begin. You are worthy of every bit of kindness and respect you offer yourself—and it's this belief that will propel you toward a life of limitless possibility.

Affirmations and Belief Systems for Confidence

Building confidence isn't an overnight process—it's a journey of reshaping how we see ourselves and the world around us. One of the most powerful tools for cultivating confidence is the use of affirmations. Affirmations are positive, powerful statements that you repeat to yourself, designed to challenge and change any negative beliefs or self-doubt that might be holding you back. When paired with a strong belief system, affirmations can create a profound shift in your mindset, helping you move from self-doubt to unshakable confidence.

1. Understanding the Power of Affirmations

At their core, affirmations are a way to reprogram your subconscious mind. We all have an internal narrative that shapes our actions, beliefs, and emotions. If that narrative is filled with negativity, fear, or self-criticism, it's difficult to act confidently. Affirmations work by providing your mind with positive, empowering thoughts to replace the limiting beliefs that have been holding you back.

The brain is wired to believe what it's repeatedly told. If you constantly affirm negative beliefs—such as "I'm not good enough" or "I always fail"—your brain will continue to interpret the world through that lens. However, when you start intentionally choosing positive affirmations, your brain begins to shift toward a mindset of possibility and strength.

For example, instead of saying, "I can't do this," an affirmation could be, "I am capable, confident, and resilient." Repeating this affirmation daily reprograms your subconscious, helping you internalize a more empowering belief about yourself.

Example: Think about a situation where you felt unprepared or unsure of yourself. Now, imagine repeating an affirmation like, "I am confident and prepared for any challenge." Over time, this affirmation will help reinforce your ability to face challenges with a sense of calm and assurance.

2. Affirmations as Tools for Confidence

Affirmations work because they help you align your thoughts with your goals. When you're striving to build your confidence, affirmations give you the opportunity to intentionally focus on your strengths, capabilities, and worth. The more you repeat positive affirmations, the more your mind begins to believe them, gradually replacing limiting beliefs with empowering ones.

When using affirmations to build confidence, it's important to focus on the present moment rather than something abstract or in the future. Instead of saying, "I will be confident," say, "I am confident." This shifts the focus to the now and helps reinforce the mindset you want to embody today.

Here are a few examples of affirmations that can enhance your confidence:

- **"I am worthy of success and happiness."**

- **"I trust in my abilities and make decisions with confidence."**

- "I am proud of who I am and the progress I've made."

- "I believe in my potential to achieve my goals."

- "I am strong, capable, and resilient in the face of challenges."

These affirmations act as reminders that you have the strength to navigate whatever comes your way and that you are deserving of success, love, and respect.

3. How Belief Systems Shape Your Confidence

Our beliefs about ourselves often stem from our past experiences, social conditioning, and messages we've received throughout our lives. These beliefs form a system that either supports or sabotages our growth. For example, if you were raised in an environment where you were constantly criticized or not encouraged to believe in yourself, you might carry those limiting beliefs into adulthood.

However, just like affirmations, beliefs can be changed. The key is to understand that beliefs are not fixed truths—they are learned patterns of thinking that can be reshaped with conscious effort and consistent practice.

A belief system that supports confidence is one where you recognize that:

- **You are enough** just as you are, regardless of external achievements or validations.

- **You are capable** of learning, growing, and overcoming challenges.

- **You deserve success and happiness**, and you're worthy of pursuing your dreams.

- **You have the power to change** your circumstances, shape your future, and create the life you desire.

To build a belief system that supports confidence, it's essential to identify and challenge any negative or limiting beliefs you hold. For instance, if you believe, "I'm not good enough to succeed," an affirmation like, "I am worthy of success" can help replace that thought.

Changing your belief system is an ongoing process. Every time you challenge a limiting belief, you reinforce a new, empowering thought. This transformation doesn't happen overnight, but with persistence, it leads to greater confidence and a more positive self-image.

Example: If you have a belief that you're not good at public speaking, use affirmations like, "I am a confident and effective communicator." Over time, as you practice these affirmations and take action, your belief system will shift, and you will start to feel more comfortable and confident when speaking in front of others.

4. Consistency is Key: Creating a Daily Affirmation Practice

To truly benefit from affirmations and shift your belief system toward confidence, consistency is key. Just as you wouldn't expect to build a muscle after one trip to the gym, you can't expect your belief system to change after a few affirmations. It takes regular, intentional practice.

A great way to incorporate affirmations into your daily routine is to make them part of your morning ritual. Start your day with affirmations that center you and reinforce your confidence. You might say them out loud in front of the mirror, write them in a journal, or simply repeat them to yourself throughout the day.

Consider setting aside 5–10 minutes each day for affirmations. During this time, focus on the meaning behind each statement, and visualize yourself embodying the qualities of confidence, strength, and resilience. Over time, these daily practices will begin to reshape your subconscious mind, gradually making confidence a natural part of who you are.

Example: You can write your affirmations in your journal each morning, repeating them with conviction. Or, you might choose to say them aloud while looking at yourself in the mirror, connecting with the emotions and self-assurance behind each statement. This process can deepen your belief in the affirmations, helping them to become a powerful tool in building lasting confidence.

5. Overcoming Resistance and Doubt

It's natural for resistance and doubt to arise when you first begin using affirmations. You might think, *"This isn't true. I don't feel confident."* This resistance is simply your mind's way of holding onto the old patterns and beliefs that no longer serve you.

Rather than ignoring or dismissing these feelings, acknowledge them. Understand that doubt is part of the process of transformation. It's a signal that you are stepping outside of your comfort zone and challenging old beliefs. With time and consistent effort, these doubts will begin to fade, and your new belief system will feel more aligned with who you truly are.

Example: When you feel doubt, remind yourself that affirmations are not about pretending or denying reality—they're about reinforcing your strengths and potential. Allow yourself to feel the discomfort of doubt without letting it hold you back. Over time, you'll notice that your affirmations begin to feel more genuine and empowering.

Conclusion: Confidence Begins from Within

Affirmations are more than just words—they are tools for creating lasting change in your belief system. When you repeat empowering affirmations, you begin to reshape your mindset, challenge limiting beliefs, and build the foundation for lasting confidence.

By consistently using affirmations and aligning them with a belief system that supports your growth, you will gradually shift from a mindset of self-doubt to one of self-assurance. Confidence doesn't come from external validation—it comes from within. And with the right mindset, you can create a life where you believe in your worth, your abilities, and your potential to achieve greatness.

Practical Step: Self-Worth Exercises

Building self-worth is a transformative process that requires intentional practice. The way we perceive ourselves shapes our confidence, relationships, and ability to pursue our dreams. When we feel worthy, we step into our power and embrace life's opportunities with boldness and clarity. But how do we begin to shift from self-doubt to self-worth? The answer lies in consistent, actionable steps—exercises that help reinforce our value and remind us of our inherent strengths. Here are some practical exercises you can implement to build and nurture your self-worth.

1. Write a Self-Worth Affirmation Statement

One of the simplest and most effective exercises to begin building your self-worth is to create a personal affirmation statement. This is a positive, empowering sentence that reflects your inherent value and capabilities. The key to crafting a strong affirmation is to focus on your strengths, qualities, and values, not external accomplishments.

Example Affirmation:

"I am worthy of love, success, and happiness. I trust my abilities and honor my worth."

Once you've written your affirmation, repeat it daily—especially in the morning before you start your day. As you say the affirmation aloud, feel the truth of the words resonate within you. Your subconscious mind will begin to internalize the affirmation, slowly shifting your self-perception toward greater self-worth.

Action:
Write your own self-worth affirmation statement and place it somewhere visible—on your mirror, in your journal, or as a reminder on your phone. Say it to yourself every day, with conviction, and truly feel the words.

2. List Your Strengths and Achievements

Our natural tendency is often to focus on what we don't have or what we've failed at. This exercise is meant to reverse that habit by helping you recognize all the amazing qualities and accomplishments that make you unique and capable.

Action:
Take a moment to list your strengths—skills, talents, personality traits, and values. What are you good at? What do others appreciate about you? Next, write down your accomplishments—big and small. Did you complete a project? Did you help someone in need? Did you overcome a challenge? Every success, no matter how small, is evidence of your worth.

Tip: Keep this list visible—add to it whenever you achieve something new, no matter how small. The more you focus on your strengths, the more your self-worth will grow.

3. Practice Self-Compassion Through Self-Care

Self-worth and self-compassion go hand-in-hand. When we treat ourselves with kindness and care, we reinforce the message that we are worthy of love and respect. Practicing self-care doesn't just mean pampering yourself physically (though that's part of it!). It's also about acknowledging your emotional, mental, and spiritual needs.

Action:
Start by scheduling time each week for self-care activities that nourish your mind, body, and spirit. This could be something simple like taking a walk, reading a book that inspires you, practicing yoga, journaling, or simply taking time to relax. Make self-care a regular part of your routine, as it signals to yourself that you deserve to feel good and be well.

Tip: If you're feeling particularly stressed or low, take five minutes to engage in a self-compassion practice. Put your hand over your heart, breathe deeply, and say something loving to yourself, such as, "I am doing my best, and I am enough." This small act can reframe your mindset and help you reconnect with your inner worth.

4. Identify and Challenge Negative Self-Talk

Our internal dialogue plays a powerful role in shaping our self-worth. If we're constantly criticizing ourselves, we're reinforcing the belief that we aren't good enough. The goal here is to become aware of negative self-talk and actively replace it with kinder, more supportive thoughts.

Action:
For one week, pay close attention to the thoughts you have about yourself. Are they kind and compassionate, or are they harsh and judgmental? When you catch yourself thinking something negative, challenge it. Ask yourself, "Is this thought true? Is it helpful? How can I reframe this in a more positive way?"

Example:
Negative thought: "I always mess up, I'm such a failure."

Reframed thought: "I made a mistake, but that doesn't define me. I can learn from this and do better next time."

As you practice reframing your negative self-talk, your perception of yourself will shift, reinforcing your inherent worth.

5. Visualize Your Worth and Potential

Visualization is a powerful technique that can help you feel more confident and connected to your own value. By visualizing yourself as worthy, successful, and capable, you begin to embody these qualities in your daily life.

Action:
Set aside 5–10 minutes each day to sit quietly and close your eyes. Visualize yourself standing tall, radiating self-confidence and inner strength. See yourself achieving your goals, handling challenges with ease, and receiving the love and respect you deserve. Imagine feeling proud of who you are, both inside and out. As you continue to practice this visualization, you'll begin to internalize the sense of self-worth and confidence you're cultivating.

Tip: Try adding positive affirmations to your visualization practice, such as, "I am worthy of success and happiness" or "I believe in my abilities and trust myself."

6. The Self-Worth Jar

A fun and tangible exercise to reinforce your self-worth is the "Self-Worth Jar." This simple yet impactful practice can serve as a daily reminder of your value and all the reasons you deserve to feel good about yourself.

Action:
Get a jar or a small container and a stack of small pieces of paper. Each day, write down one positive thing about yourself on a slip of paper—something you accomplished, a quality you admire in yourself, or a compliment you received. Fold the paper and place it in the jar. Over time, this jar will become a powerful visual representation of your self-worth.

Tip: When you're feeling low or in need of a confidence boost, take a moment to pull out a few slips from your jar. Read them aloud and remind yourself of all the amazing things you've done and the incredible person you are.

7. Practice Gratitude for Yourself

Gratitude is a powerful practice for shifting your mindset from scarcity to abundance. By practicing gratitude for yourself, you begin to acknowledge and appreciate all the ways in which you are deserving of love, care, and respect.

Action:
Each day, write down three things you are grateful for about yourself. This could be anything—from your resilience in tough times to the love you give to others. It could be something as simple as being grateful for your kindness, your determination, or your creativity. Focusing on what makes you grateful for yourself enhances your self-worth and helps you see the positive impact you have in the world.

Example:
"I am grateful for my ability to stay calm under pressure."

"I am grateful for the compassion I show to others."

"I am grateful for my creativity and problem-solving skills."

Conclusion: Nurturing Your Self-Worth Every Day

Building self-worth is an ongoing practice, and it requires patience and consistency. By incorporating these exercises into your daily routine, you can gradually shift your perception of yourself and embrace your inherent value. The more you focus on your strengths, acknowledge your accomplishments, and treat yourself with compassion and respect, the more your confidence will grow.

Remember, your worth isn't dependent on external achievements or validation. You are worthy because you exist, because you have a unique set of talents, qualities, and experiences that make you valuable. As you continue to nurture your self-worth, you'll create a solid foundation for a life full of confidence, growth, and limitless possibilities.

6

Learning, Growing and Moving Forward

The Fear of Failure and Its Impact on Progress

Failure. Just the word itself can send a shiver down the spine of many people. It triggers feelings of dread, embarrassment, and self-doubt. We live in a society that often measures success by perfection, instant results, and external validation. As a result, failure can feel like the end of the road—a sign that we're not good enough, not capable enough, or not worthy of success. But what if failure isn't something to fear, but something to embrace?

The fear of failure, though natural, can be one of the biggest obstacles to personal growth and progress. It holds us back from taking risks, trying new things, and pursuing our dreams. When we allow the fear of failing to dictate our actions, we inadvertently create a barrier between us and the very progress we seek. To truly move forward in life, we must first understand how the fear of failure impacts us—and how we can shift our mindset to view failure as a stepping stone rather than a roadblock.

1. The Paralysis of Perfectionism

For many, the fear of failure is closely linked to perfectionism. Perfectionism is the belief that you must do everything flawlessly, without mistakes or missteps. This mindset can be paralyzing, as it creates the belief that anything less than perfect is unacceptable. As a result, perfectionists often avoid taking risks, fearing that they won't meet their own or others' high expectations.

This fear of imperfection can stop progress in its tracks. You might hesitate to start a new project, apply for a job, or pursue a goal because you're terrified that you won't do it perfectly. And in doing so, you miss out on the opportunity to learn, grow, and improve. Ironically, perfectionism often leads to stagnation rather than success.

Action:

Recognize that perfection is an illusion. Mistakes and imperfections are part of the journey to success. Shift your mindset from aiming for flawlessness to aiming for progress. Instead of focusing on avoiding mistakes, focus on taking action and learning from each step. Embrace the idea that failure is simply feedback.

2. Fear of Judgment and Rejection

Another reason why the fear of failure is so powerful is the fear of judgment and rejection. Many people avoid pursuing their goals because they fear how others will perceive them if they fail. Whether it's a fear of disappointing family members, colleagues, or friends, or a fear of being judged by society, the thought of failure can be overwhelming when we believe it will result in harsh criticism or exclusion.

This fear can prevent us from even trying. We may hold back from expressing our true selves, sharing our ideas, or taking bold actions simply to avoid potential rejection. But by letting fear of judgment control us, we unknowingly sacrifice the very opportunities that could lead to growth and success.

Action:

Understand that everyone experiences failure. It is a universal part of life. Instead of fearing judgment, shift your focus to your personal growth and the lessons you can learn from each experience. Realize that those who judge you are often not as concerned with your failures as you think. Most people are more focused on their own lives than on critiquing yours. And, importantly, the people who truly matter will support your efforts, no matter the outcome.

3. The Limiting Belief of "Failure Defines Me"

When you fear failure, it's easy to fall into the trap of believing that failure defines who you are as a person. If you fail, you think, *"I'm a failure."* This belief is deeply damaging, as it ties your self-worth directly to your outcomes. It becomes easy to see failure as a reflection of your inadequacy rather than as a temporary setback.

The truth is, failure doesn't define who you are. It's just a part of the journey—a necessary stepping stone on the path to success. Every person who has ever achieved greatness has failed at some point. The difference is that they didn't allow failure to dictate their self-worth. Instead, they saw it as an opportunity to learn, improve, and grow stronger.

Action:
Start separating your identity from your outcomes. Remind yourself that failure is not a reflection of your worth, but a natural part of growth. Instead of saying, *"I failed,"* try saying, *"I experienced a setback, but I can learn from it and keep moving forward."* Shift your mindset to see failure as an event, not an identity.

4. The Impact on Creativity and Innovation

The fear of failure also limits creativity and innovation. When we fear failure, we often avoid trying new things or thinking outside the box because we're afraid that the outcome will be less than perfect. This fear can stifle our creativity and prevent us from exploring new ideas, taking risks, or experimenting with different approaches. As a result, we limit ourselves to what feels safe and familiar—yet, this is often where growth and innovation lie.

In reality, the most groundbreaking ideas and innovations often come from taking risks and embracing failure as part of the creative process. Thomas Edison famously said, *"I have not failed. I've just found 10,000 ways that won't work."* The path to success is often paved with trial and error, and embracing this process allows for the freedom to experiment and create without the burden of perfection.

Action:
Give yourself permission to be creative and take risks without worrying about the end result. Focus on the process, not the outcome. Allow yourself to fail, knowing that each failure brings you closer to finding a solution or creating something meaningful. Celebrate the learning that comes from every attempt.

5. How the Fear of Failure Limits Our Potential

Ultimately, the fear of failure limits our potential by keeping us stuck in a cycle of inaction. We procrastinate, avoid challenges, or play it safe because we are afraid of what might happen if we fail. But by doing so, we miss out on the opportunities for growth and success that lie on the other side of failure.

Failure is not something to be feared; it is something to be welcomed. It's the teacher that guides us, the experience that shapes us, and the momentum that pushes us toward progress. When we change our relationship with failure, we open ourselves up to the limitless potential within us.

Action:
Start viewing failure as an opportunity to grow rather than a setback. Embrace it as a teacher, an essential part of the process that helps you refine your skills, sharpen your focus, and develop resilience. Each time you fail, ask yourself, *"What can I learn from this?"* and use that lesson to propel yourself forward.

Conclusion: Letting Go of the Fear of Failure

The fear of failure is natural, but it doesn't have to hold you back. By understanding how it impacts your progress, you can begin to shift your mindset and embrace failure as a vital part of the growth process. When you stop seeing failure as something to fear and start seeing it as a stepping stone to success, you'll unlock your true potential.

Remember, every great success story includes moments of failure. The difference between those who succeed and those who don't is simple: the willingness to keep going in the face of failure, to learn from mistakes, and to grow stronger with each setback. Let go of the fear, take bold action, and keep moving forward. Your success is on the other side of failure—waiting for you to embrace it.

Challenging the Narrative: Failure as a Stepping Stone to Success

We've all heard it before: "Failure is not an option." Society often tells us that success comes with perfection, and that failure is something to be avoided at all costs. But what if we've been taught to fear failure for all the wrong reasons? What if failure isn't a sign of defeat but actually a crucial part of the path to success?

Challenging the traditional narrative about failure is one of the most powerful shifts we can make on our journey of growth. When we reframe failure from something shameful to something valuable, we open ourselves up to new opportunities, lessons, and progress. Instead of seeing failure as a roadblock, we can view it as a vital stepping stone—a necessary part of the process of achieving anything worthwhile.

1. The Myth of Overnight Success

One of the most damaging myths about success is the idea that it happens overnight or with a single, flawless effort. We look at successful people, from entrepreneurs to artists to athletes, and see their accomplishments as the result of luck, talent, or a perfect formula. What we don't always see are the countless failures, setbacks, and lessons learned along the way.

In reality, every success story is built on a foundation of trial and error, mistakes, and perseverance. Thomas Edison, whose name is synonymous with invention, famously failed over 1,000 times before successfully inventing the lightbulb. His own words say it all: *"I have not failed. I've just found 10,000 ways that won't work."*

The difference between those who achieve greatness and those who don't isn't avoiding failure—it's the willingness to continue despite it. When we change the narrative, we stop seeing failure as a reflection of our inadequacy and start seeing it as the inevitable part of learning and growth.

Action:

Next time you experience a setback or failure, instead of asking, *"What went wrong?"* ask, *"What can I learn from this?"* This shift in perspective will help you view failure as a lesson, not a defeat.

2. Failure is Not Permanent—It's Part of the Process

Failure is often perceived as a permanent state—a label we fear we will wear forever. We think, *"If I fail this project, I am a failure. If I don't succeed now, I will never succeed."* But this narrative is misleading. In reality, failure is rarely permanent. It's simply a part of the process of growth and development.

Failure means that something didn't work—whether it's a strategy, an idea, or an action. But it doesn't mean you are incapable of achieving success. It doesn't define you. Some of the world's greatest innovations came from people who faced multiple failures before finding the right approach. The key is to stay in the game, continue to adjust, and never give up.

Think about the famous phrase, *"Fall seven times, stand up eight."* It speaks to the resilience required to push through failure and move forward. When we view failure as a temporary roadblock rather than a permanent defeat, it becomes something we can overcome rather than something that stops us.

Action:

Shift your mindset around failure by reminding yourself that it is a temporary setback, not a permanent state. After each failure, give yourself permission to pause, reflect, learn, and then take action again. You will see progress as long as you continue moving forward.

3. Failure Teaches Resilience and Adaptability

One of the most powerful lessons failure offers is resilience—the ability to bounce back from adversity. In life, things won't always go as planned. We can't control every outcome, and setbacks are inevitable. However, it's how we respond to failure that determines our success.

Failure teaches us to adapt, refine our approach, and become more resourceful. Each failure forces us to reassess, recalibrate, and adjust our mindset. Through this process, we become stronger, more flexible, and more capable of handling challenges in the future.

When we approach failure with a mindset of learning and adaptation, we build resilience—an essential skill for long-term success. Rather than seeing failure as an end, we begin to see it as a powerful teacher that strengthens our resolve and enhances our ability to navigate the complexities of life.

Action:
The next time you face a failure, ask yourself: *"What can I do differently? How can I adjust my approach to move forward?"* This will help you view failure as a tool for developing greater resilience and adaptability.

4. Success Is Not a Linear Path—It's Full of Twists and Turns

The journey to success is rarely straightforward. We all have an idea of where we want to go, but the path is often winding and full of unexpected challenges. If we view success as a straight line, we set ourselves up for disappointment and frustration. The reality is that success is often built on detours, setbacks, and course corrections.

Failure is just one of those inevitable detours. It's a part of the messy, unpredictable process of reaching our goals. By embracing failure as part of the journey, we stop trying to control every outcome and start allowing ourselves to grow through the challenges. We begin to see setbacks not as failures, but as the necessary experiences that help us refine our approach and build a deeper understanding of our purpose.

Action:
Embrace the idea that success doesn't happen in a straight line. Understand that each twist, turn, and failure is part of the journey and has something valuable to teach you. Stay flexible and open to learning from every experience.

5. Rewriting the Story: Failure Is a Stepping Stone to Success

The most transformative shift we can make is to change how we view failure. Instead of seeing it as a roadblock, we need to start seeing it as an opportunity—an essential stepping stone on the path to success. Failure provides feedback, teaches lessons, and offers the chance to try again with more knowledge and wisdom than before.

The stories we tell ourselves about failure often shape our reality. If we tell ourselves that failure means we're not good enough or we'll never succeed, we create a self-fulfilling prophecy. But if we tell ourselves that failure is a natural part of growth and success, we unlock our potential to achieve great things.

Action:
Reframe the narrative around failure. The next time you experience a setback, remind yourself that it is not a reflection of your worth but a necessary part of the process. Embrace the failure, learn from it, and move forward with renewed energy and determination.

Conclusion: Embracing Failure as a Stepping Stone

When we stop fearing failure and start embracing it as a stepping stone to success, everything changes. We free ourselves from the burden of perfectionism and self-doubt. We open ourselves up to taking risks, trying new things, and learning from every experience.

Failure is not the opposite of success—it's a key component of it. It's the place where we gain wisdom, build resilience, and refine our strategies. So, challenge the narrative. Instead of seeing failure as something to avoid, see it for what it truly is: an essential part of the journey to success. The next time you encounter failure, remember—it's not the end. It's just the beginning of your next great leap forward.

How to Reframe Setbacks as Lessons

Setbacks are a natural part of life. They can feel frustrating, disheartening, and even discouraging at times. Whether it's a project that didn't go as planned, an opportunity that slipped through your fingers, or a goal that feels just out of reach, setbacks have a way of testing our resolve. But what if, instead of seeing setbacks as failures or obstacles, we could reframe them as lessons—valuable experiences that contribute to our growth and success?

Reframing setbacks is a powerful tool in transforming our mindset. It allows us to view challenges not as roadblocks, but as opportunities for learning, improvement, and self-discovery. When we shift our perspective on setbacks, we stop feeling defeated by them and start feeling empowered to move forward with greater wisdom and clarity.

1. Understand That Setbacks Are Part of the Process

One of the most important things to recognize is that setbacks are not abnormal. They are a natural part of any growth process. If you've ever set out to learn something new, build a career, or pursue a meaningful goal, you know that there are going to be bumps along the way. Success is rarely linear, and failure or setbacks are simply part of the journey.

When we understand that setbacks are a natural part of growth, we stop viewing them as catastrophic or insurmountable. Instead, we can embrace them as a necessary element of progress. Just like a seed needs to push through the soil to grow into a plant, our setbacks help us grow stronger, more resilient, and more knowledgeable.

Action:
Next time you face a setback, remind yourself that this is part of the process. Instead of feeling discouraged, see it as a sign that you are moving forward and learning along the way.

2. Ask Yourself: "What Can I Learn from This?"

When faced with a setback, it's easy to get caught up in emotions like frustration or disappointment. However, the key to reframing a setback as a lesson is to take a step back and ask yourself: *"What can I learn from this?"*

Every setback offers valuable insights, even if it's not immediately obvious. Perhaps you learned that a certain strategy didn't work, that you were too focused on the wrong goal, or that your timing was off. Maybe the setback revealed something about your approach, your mindset, or your emotional resilience. By asking the right questions, you can uncover the lessons hidden within the setback.

Action:
When you experience a setback, take a moment to reflect and ask, *"What can I learn from this?"* Write down your insights and use them to adjust your strategy moving forward. This simple exercise helps you turn any setback into a valuable lesson.

3. Shift from Blame to Curiosity

It's easy to slip into a pattern of self-blame when things don't go as planned. You might think, *"I messed up,"* or *"I'm not good enough."* But self-blame only keeps you stuck in negative emotions and prevents you from learning from the experience.

Instead of blaming yourself or others, approach setbacks with curiosity. Be curious about what went wrong, what you could have done differently, and how you can improve next time. Curiosity opens up a space for growth and exploration, allowing you to see setbacks as opportunities for refinement rather than failures.

Action:
Next time a setback occurs, replace self-blame with curiosity. Ask yourself, *"What did I learn? How can I improve?"* Cultivating curiosity will help you shift from a fixed mindset to a growth mindset, enabling you to see every setback as a valuable lesson.

4. Reframe Your Narrative: "I Haven't Failed; I've Gained Experience"

The way you talk to yourself about setbacks is incredibly important. If you view a setback as a failure, it can have a significant impact on your motivation and confidence. However, if you reframe your narrative and tell yourself that you haven't failed—you've gained valuable experience—you can shift your mindset to one of growth and empowerment.

Every time you face a setback, remind yourself that you've learned something new. Even if the outcome wasn't what you expected, you've gained knowledge that will help you in the future. This shift in narrative helps you detach your self-worth from the outcome and refocus on the learning process.

Action:
Start rewriting your internal dialogue about setbacks. Instead of saying, *"I failed,"* say, *"I gained valuable experience that will help me succeed next time."* This small shift in thinking can change the way you approach challenges in the future.

5. Embrace the Long-Term Vision

It's easy to get caught up in the short-term frustrations of a setback. You might be tempted to judge your entire journey based on one obstacle. But remember, success is a long-term game. Setbacks don't define the whole story; they are just chapters within a larger narrative.

By embracing the long-term vision, you allow setbacks to be just one part of the bigger picture. A single setback doesn't diminish your overall progress or potential. When you zoom out and focus on your bigger goals, setbacks become less daunting and more manageable.

Action:
Whenever you experience a setback, remind yourself of the long-term vision. Ask, *"How does this setback fit into my larger journey?"* By keeping the big picture in mind, you'll be able to navigate setbacks with a sense of perspective and purpose.

6. Use Setbacks to Build Resilience

Setbacks are also an opportunity to build emotional resilience. Every time you face a challenge and choose to persevere, you strengthen your capacity to cope with adversity. It's like building muscle: the more you exercise it, the stronger it gets.

Rather than allowing setbacks to discourage you, embrace them as an opportunity to become more resilient. Each challenge you overcome adds to your ability to handle future obstacles with greater ease and confidence. The resilience you build during setbacks will serve you well in both personal and professional growth.

Action:

When you experience a setback, focus on how it's helping you become more resilient. Remind yourself of past challenges you've overcome and how they've made you stronger. This will shift your mindset and empower you to keep moving forward, no matter the challenge.

Conclusion: Setbacks as Stepping Stones

Reframing setbacks as lessons is one of the most powerful ways to turn challenges into opportunities for growth. By viewing setbacks not as failures but as stepping stones on the path to success, you empower yourself to learn, adapt, and become stronger with each experience.

Instead of fearing setbacks, embrace them as a necessary part of your journey. Every setback offers a lesson that can propel you toward your next success. The more you can reframe your setbacks as opportunities to learn, grow, and improve, the more you will unlock your true potential and move closer to your goals. Remember: setbacks are not the end of the road—they are just detours leading you to something greater.

Building Resilience Through Mindset Shifts

Resilience is not something we are born with; it's something we develop over time through our responses to challenges and setbacks. It's the ability to bounce back from adversity, to keep going when things get tough, and to stay strong in the face of difficulties. While some people seem to naturally possess a resilient attitude, the truth is that resilience is largely shaped by the way we think. Our mindset plays a critical role in determining whether we view challenges as obstacles or opportunities.

By making specific mindset shifts, we can actively build our resilience and strengthen our ability to cope with life's ups and downs. These mindset shifts are powerful tools that can help us face adversity with greater confidence, determination, and flexibility. When we change the way we perceive and react to hardship, we equip ourselves with the mental strength needed to persevere and thrive.

1. Embrace a Growth Mindset

One of the most important mindset shifts for building resilience is adopting a **growth mindset**. This concept, introduced by psychologist Carol Dweck, is based on the belief that our abilities and intelligence can be developed through hard work, perseverance, and learning. A growth mindset sees challenges not as threats, but as opportunities to grow.

When faced with adversity, someone with a growth mindset doesn't see it as a sign of failure. Instead, they view it as a learning experience—something that will help them improve. With this mindset, setbacks are no longer seen as the end, but rather as the beginning of a new lesson and a chance to do better next time.

Action:
The next time you face a challenge, remind yourself that growth happens through effort and learning. Rather than focusing on the difficulty or the setback, focus on what you can learn from the experience and how it can help you improve moving forward.

2. Reframe Adversity as a Challenge, Not a Threat

How we view adversity plays a crucial role in how we respond to it. If we see challenges as insurmountable threats, we become paralyzed by fear and doubt. On the other hand, when we view adversity as a **challenge** to overcome, we approach it with problem-solving skills, creativity, and determination.

This mindset shift helps us remain calm and focused in tough situations. Instead of becoming overwhelmed or discouraged, we ask ourselves, *"What can I do to overcome this? How can I approach this challenge in a way that will help me grow?"* Viewing adversity as a challenge reaffirms our belief in our ability to handle difficult situations and reinforces the idea that we can always find a way forward.

Action:
When you encounter a difficult situation, consciously choose to see it as a challenge rather than a threat. Ask yourself, *"How can I handle this with grace and*

determination?" Shift your thinking to one that sees obstacles as puzzles waiting to be solved.

3. Cultivate Self-Compassion Instead of Self-Criticism

When life gets tough, it's easy to fall into the trap of **self-criticism**. We often blame ourselves for mistakes or judge ourselves harshly when things don't go as planned. This negative self-talk only weakens our resilience and makes it harder to recover from setbacks.

Building resilience requires **self-compassion**—the ability to treat ourselves with kindness, understanding, and patience when we face difficulties. Instead of beating ourselves up, we acknowledge that setbacks are a part of life, and we offer ourselves the same compassion we would offer a friend going through a tough time. Self-compassion helps us to process failure without letting it diminish our self-worth.

Action:
Whenever you make a mistake or face a challenge, practice self-compassion. Speak to yourself as you would to someone you love. Remind yourself that it's okay to make mistakes, and use them as opportunities to learn and grow, not as reasons to be harsh on yourself.

4. Focus on What You Can Control

One of the hallmarks of resilient people is their ability to focus on what they can control, rather than worrying about what they can't. Life is full of uncertainties, and there are many things beyond our control. But we always have control over our attitudes, our actions, and our responses to situations.

Instead of spending energy on what's outside of your control—like other people's reactions or circumstances—focus on what you can influence. This shift allows you to feel empowered and proactive, even in the midst of adversity. When you focus on actionable steps, you regain a sense of control and start to move forward, no matter how challenging the situation may seem.

Action:

In moments of stress or challenge, pause and identify what aspects of the situation you can control. Is it your mindset? Your response? Your actions? Focus your energy on those things, and let go of what you cannot influence.

5. Cultivate Patience and Persistence

Building resilience also requires **patience**—the patience to understand that not every obstacle can be overcome immediately, and that setbacks don't mean you've failed. Resilient people know that progress takes time. They stay committed to their goals, even when things are difficult or don't happen quickly.

Persistence, coupled with patience, creates a powerful combination. Instead of giving up when things get tough, resilient people push through the discomfort, knowing that every small step forward counts. They understand that resilience isn't about avoiding failure, but about continuing to move forward even in the face of it.

Action:

When you feel like giving up, remind yourself of the power of patience and persistence. Break your goals into smaller, manageable steps and commit to taking one step at a time. Trust that, with each effort, you are moving closer to your desired outcome.

6. Practice Gratitude in Difficult Times

It might seem counterintuitive, but **gratitude** is one of the most effective ways to build resilience. When we practice gratitude—especially during challenging times—we shift our focus from what's going wrong to what's going right. This shift in perspective not only boosts our mood but also strengthens our ability to bounce back.

Gratitude helps us to reframe adversity and see it in a new light. It reminds us that even in tough situations, there are things to be thankful for: lessons learned, personal growth, or even the support of loved ones. By consciously practicing gratitude, we increase our emotional resources and strengthen our capacity for resilience.

Action:

In times of difficulty, take a moment each day to write down three things you're grateful for. Whether they are big or small, focusing on the positives can help shift your mindset and boost your resilience.

Conclusion: Resilience is a Skill, Not a Trait

Building resilience is not about avoiding hardship—it's about how we respond to it. By shifting our mindset, we empower ourselves to face challenges with courage, adaptability, and determination. Every setback becomes an opportunity for growth, every challenge a chance to become stronger.

Remember, resilience is a skill that can be developed, and it starts with how we choose to think. When we embrace a growth mindset, reframe adversity as a challenge, practice self-compassion, focus on what we can control, remain patient and persistent, and cultivate gratitude, we build the mental strength needed to navigate life's inevitable ups and downs. These mindset shifts don't just help us bounce back—they help us move forward with greater strength, clarity, and confidence.

Practical Step: Creating a Failure-to-Success Roadmap

When you set out to achieve something meaningful, the road to success often isn't a straight line. Instead, it's filled with twists, turns, setbacks, and unexpected challenges. Understanding that failure is an integral part of success allows you to embrace those moments and use them as stepping stones. One of the most effective ways to do this is by creating a **Failure-to-Success Roadmap**—a strategic plan that helps you navigate setbacks, learn from them, and ultimately transform them into opportunities for growth.

The Failure-to-Success Roadmap is a tool that empowers you to approach your goals with a mindset of resilience, learning, and adaptability. It's a way to turn the inevitable failures into fuel for success, allowing you to bounce back stronger, smarter, and more determined.

1. Define Your End Goal

Before you can create a roadmap, you first need to define where you want to go. What does success look like for you? Whether it's a career milestone, personal development goal, or a specific achievement, clearly articulating your desired outcome gives you direction and purpose. The more specific your goal, the clearer your roadmap will be.

Action:

Take a few moments to write down your ultimate goal. Make it specific and measurable. Ask yourself, *"What does success look like, and why is it important to me?"* This clarity will guide you as you create your roadmap.

2. Identify Potential Failures Along the Way

This step might seem counterintuitive, but it's critical for your success. Recognizing potential setbacks before they happen helps you to anticipate challenges and prepare for them. Think about the obstacles you might face— whether they are external (like financial challenges, lack of resources, or other people's opinions) or internal (like self-doubt, fear of failure, or procrastination). Identifying these potential failures allows you to develop strategies to either avoid or cope with them when they arise.

Action:

Make a list of potential setbacks or obstacles that could arise on your path to success. Don't focus solely on the negative, but try to think realistically about the challenges you might face. Consider both internal and external factors that could get in your way.

3. Reframe Each Setback as a Learning Opportunity

Now that you've identified possible failures, the next step is to reframe them. Instead of seeing each obstacle as a dead-end, consider how you can learn and grow from it. Every failure is an opportunity to gain valuable insight, whether it's discovering a new strategy, understanding your limitations, or realizing a personal strength. By changing your mindset and viewing setbacks as lessons, you transform them from roadblocks into building blocks.

Action:

For each potential setback you've listed, write down how you can turn it into a learning opportunity. What could you learn from the experience? What action can you take to grow from it? For example, if you face a financial setback, the lesson might be that you need to budget more carefully or seek additional funding.

4. Break Down the Roadmap into Actionable Steps

Success doesn't happen in one giant leap. It's the result of small, consistent actions over time. The key to turning setbacks into successes is breaking your journey down into smaller, actionable steps. This helps you stay focused, build momentum, and avoid feeling overwhelmed by the bigger picture. Each small step is a victory that gets you closer to your goal, and even if you encounter setbacks along the way, the smaller actions give you the confidence to keep going.

Action:

Break down your larger goal into smaller, manageable tasks. Create a timeline or schedule for accomplishing these steps, and set realistic milestones along the way. Even when setbacks occur, having a clear plan will keep you focused on moving forward.

5. Create a Plan for Managing Setbacks

It's essential to have a plan for how to manage setbacks when they occur. This is where resilience comes in. When things go wrong, having a pre-established action plan will prevent you from feeling lost or discouraged. Your plan might include self-care strategies, accountability partners, or resources to help you regain focus. The key is to have a set of tools in place so that when you face setbacks, you know exactly what to do next.

Action:

Develop a plan for handling setbacks. This could involve taking a short break to regain perspective, journaling to reflect on the situation, reaching out to a mentor for advice, or revising your approach based on new insights. Having these tools ready will help you stay calm and focused during tough times.

6. Track Your Progress and Adjust Your Strategy

One of the most powerful aspects of the Failure-to-Success Roadmap is the ability to **track your progress**. As you move forward, it's important to regularly evaluate how you're doing. Are you staying on track? Are there areas where you need to adjust your approach? Progress is rarely linear, and setbacks can sometimes lead to unexpected detours. By tracking your progress, you stay adaptable and ready to make necessary adjustments to your plan.

Action:
Set up a system to track your progress. This could be a weekly check-in or a more structured tracking tool, such as a journal or a digital planner. Review your progress, assess any setbacks, and adjust your strategy as needed. The ability to adapt quickly will ensure that setbacks don't derail your ultimate success.

7. Celebrate Small Wins Along the Way

It's easy to get caught up in the bigger picture and forget to celebrate the small victories that happen along the way. These small wins are crucial for building momentum and maintaining motivation. Each time you overcome a setback or accomplish a step in your roadmap, take time to acknowledge your progress. This celebration will reinforce your belief in your ability to succeed and help you maintain the positive energy you need to keep moving forward.

Action:
Celebrate your small wins. Whether it's completing a difficult task, learning from a setback, or simply staying consistent, take a moment to appreciate your progress. These celebrations will fuel your motivation and remind you that you are on the right path.

Conclusion: The Roadmap to Success Is Built Through Failure

Creating a Failure-to-Success Roadmap is a powerful way to navigate challenges with confidence and clarity. By identifying potential setbacks, reframing them as learning opportunities, breaking down your goal into actionable steps, and having a plan for managing adversity, you can stay focused on your ultimate goal—no matter how many failures you encounter along the way.

Remember, failure is not the opposite of success; it is a vital part of the journey. By viewing each setback as a lesson rather than a defeat, you build resilience and develop the mental strength needed to push forward. Your roadmap is not just about avoiding failure—it's about embracing it as a stepping stone to success. Keep moving, keep learning, and keep growing. Success is the result of persistent effort, strategic planning, and a mindset that turns failure into an invaluable part of the process.

7

Shifting from Scarcity to Abundance Thinking

Understanding the Scarcity Mindset and Its Limits

The way we think shapes the reality we live in. Our mindset acts as a lens through which we perceive the world, interpret events, and make decisions. When we operate from a **scarcity mindset**, we view the world as limited, where resources—whether they are time, money, opportunities, or even love—are finite and must be competed for. This perception can create feelings of fear, anxiety, and a constant sense of lack, which in turn can limit our potential for growth and happiness.

At its core, the **scarcity mindset** is the belief that there isn't enough to go around, and that we are in constant competition with others for what's available. This belief often manifests in various aspects of life—whether it's struggling to make ends meet financially, feeling as though there's never enough time to get everything done, or believing that success is a limited resource only accessible to a select few. When we believe in scarcity, we focus on what we don't have, what we're missing, and what others are taking away from us, rather than appreciating the abundance already present in our lives.

The Characteristics of the Scarcity Mindset

People who operate from a scarcity mindset often exhibit certain behaviors or attitudes. These can include:

1. **Fear of Missing Out (FOMO):** There's an underlying fear that if we don't act quickly, we'll miss out on something important—whether that's an opportunity, a promotion, or a limited resource. This creates a sense of

urgency and pressure that can lead to stress, anxiety, and poor decision-making.

2. **Comparison with Others:** Scarcity thinking often leads to constant comparison with others. If you believe there's not enough to go around, you may view other people's successes as a reflection of your own shortcomings. You might feel jealous, envious, or threatened by others' achievements, assuming that their success takes away from your own potential.

3. **Focus on What You Lack:** The scarcity mindset keeps you focused on what you don't have rather than what you do. It creates a constant cycle of dissatisfaction and discontent, because there's always something missing—whether it's money, status, resources, or time. This can lead to frustration and a feeling that no matter how hard you try, you'll never have enough.

4. **Self-Doubt and Limiting Beliefs:** Scarcity thinking can also create self-doubt. If you believe there isn't enough success, wealth, or opportunity to go around, you may convince yourself that you're not deserving of these things. This belief can hinder personal growth, making you feel unworthy of pursuing your dreams or reaching your full potential.

5. **Clinging to the Familiar:** When you believe there is a limited amount of opportunity or resources, you may cling to what you already know, even if it's no longer serving you. The scarcity mindset keeps you stuck in fear, preventing you from embracing new opportunities, taking risks, or exploring new possibilities that could lead to growth.

The Impact of the Scarcity Mindset on Your Life

The scarcity mindset has a profound effect on how you experience life. By constantly focusing on what's missing, it limits your ability to see opportunities, recognize abundance, and create positive change. Some of the ways this mindset can affect your life include:

1. **Stagnation and Missed Opportunities:** The scarcity mindset keeps you focused on the limitations, making it difficult to see potential opportunities. Fear and doubt prevent you from taking risks, and as a result, you may miss out on chances for growth, success, and happiness.

2. **Strained Relationships:** When you view relationships through the lens of scarcity, it's easy to fall into patterns of jealousy, competition, and resentment. Whether it's feeling envious of a friend's success or worrying about someone "taking" what you have, the scarcity mindset can create tension and undermine the strength of your connections.

3. **Increased Stress and Anxiety:** The constant worry about not having enough—whether it's money, time, energy, or success—creates a chronic sense of stress. You're always focused on what you're lacking, which keeps you in a state of anxiety, fear, and overwhelm. This mental state drains your energy and prevents you from enjoying the present moment.

4. **Undermining Confidence:** When you believe there's a finite amount of success or resources, you may start doubting your own abilities and worth. The belief that others have more than you can lead to feelings of inadequacy and low self-esteem. You may hold yourself back from pursuing opportunities, fearing that you won't succeed or that there's no room for you at the table.

5. **Reinforcing Negative Patterns:** The scarcity mindset can create a cycle of negativity. When you constantly focus on what you don't have, you feed feelings of lack and dissatisfaction. This can make it harder to take positive action, as you're trapped in a loop of negativity, making it more difficult to break free and move forward.

Breaking Free from the Scarcity Mindset

While the scarcity mindset can be deeply ingrained, it's important to recognize that **it is not a permanent state of being**. By understanding the limits of scarcity thinking, you can begin to shift your mindset toward abundance. The key is recognizing that your thoughts shape your reality. When you shift your focus from lack to abundance, you open yourself up to new possibilities, increased creativity, and greater satisfaction in all areas of your life.

In the next sections of this chapter, we'll explore how you can begin to transform your thinking, embrace abundance, and start experiencing life from a place of possibility rather than limitation. But first, it's important to fully acknowledge how deeply the scarcity mindset has shaped your worldview. Once you understand its effects, you're in a stronger position to make the conscious choice to shift toward an abundance-driven perspective that opens doors to limitless potential.

The Abundance Mindset: A Game-Changer for Success

The shift from a scarcity mindset to an **abundance mindset** is not just a small change in perspective—it is a profound transformation that can completely alter the trajectory of your life. The abundance mindset is rooted in the belief that there is more than enough for everyone: more opportunities, more love, more success, and more resources. This shift moves us from a place of competition and fear to one of collaboration, possibility, and growth.

When you adopt an abundance mindset, you begin to see the world through a different lens. Instead of focusing on what you lack, you start focusing on the opportunities available to you. You become more open to new experiences, more creative in solving problems, and more confident in your ability to succeed. The abundance mindset isn't about wishful thinking; it's about consciously cultivating a sense of possibility and prosperity in every area of your life. This mindset has the power to change everything—from your relationships and career to your personal growth and overall sense of fulfilment.

Key Characteristics of the Abundance Mindset

1. **Belief in Unlimited Opportunities**

   An abundance mindset sees opportunities everywhere. People with this mindset believe that success isn't a zero-sum game; one person's gain doesn't mean another's loss. Instead of viewing the world as a place of limited resources, they recognize that there are endless possibilities to create and achieve. Whether it's career growth, creative endeavors, or personal relationships, they trust that there are always opportunities available to them.

2. Collaboration Over Competition

Rather than competing for the same resources or recognition, those with an abundance mindset embrace collaboration. They recognize that the success of others doesn't diminish their own. Instead of viewing others as rivals, they see them as potential partners and collaborators. This mindset fosters stronger, more supportive relationships, where people lift each other up, share knowledge, and work together toward mutual success.

3. Gratitude for What You Have

At the core of an abundance mindset is gratitude. People with this mindset focus on the wealth they already have in their lives—not just in terms of material wealth, but also in terms of love, health, knowledge, and experiences. Gratitude shifts their focus from lack to plenty, helping them feel fulfilled and at peace in the present moment. It also strengthens their ability to manifest more of what they want because they are energetically aligned with positivity and abundance.

4. Optimism About the Future

An abundance mindset is future-focused. People who embrace abundance believe that their best days are ahead of them. They don't let setbacks or challenges define their potential. Instead, they approach challenges as opportunities to grow and learn. They are confident that they can handle whatever life throws their way because they see every obstacle as part of a larger journey toward success.

5. Openness to Growth and Learning

Those with an abundance mindset are committed to personal growth. They believe that there is always room to expand their knowledge, skills, and potential. They are not limited by past experiences or failures; instead, they embrace a growth-oriented approach that allows them to continuously improve. This openness to learning also helps them adapt more easily to change and innovation, keeping them flexible and forward-thinking.

6. Generosity and Sharing

People with an abundance mindset are generous, not just with their resources but also with their time, attention, and support. They believe that by sharing what they have, they are contributing to a larger network of well-being and success. This generosity doesn't mean giving until you're empty—it's about understanding that the more you give, the more you receive in return, whether it's knowledge, energy, or opportunity.

The Impact of the Abundance Mindset on Success

The abundance mindset is a game-changer because it **removes the barriers that hold you back**. When you operate from a place of abundance, you are no longer limited by fear or self-doubt. Instead of focusing on potential failures, you focus on potential successes. This mindset propels you forward by shifting your energy toward growth, possibility, and action.

1. **Increased Confidence and Empowerment**

   The abundance mindset empowers you to take bold steps toward your goals. You no longer worry about whether there's enough room for you to succeed. Instead, you believe that there is always space for your unique contribution. This confidence allows you to pursue opportunities with passion and determination, knowing that you have the resources and mindset to make it happen.

2. **More Creativity and Innovation**

   When you see the world as abundant, you open yourself up to new ideas, innovative solutions, and creative thinking. You're less constrained by traditional approaches and more willing to think outside the box. The abundance mindset fuels creativity because you are free from the fear of failure. You know that even if your ideas don't work out, there are infinite other possibilities to explore.

3. **Stronger Relationships and Network**

   An abundance mindset fosters deeper, more genuine relationships. Instead of seeing others as competition, you see them as allies, collaborators, and mentors. This shift creates stronger, more supportive connections, where people are eager to help and uplift one another. This mindset also makes you more approachable and open, attracting positive, success-oriented individuals into your network.

4. **Attracting Opportunities**

When you operate from a mindset of abundance, you become a magnet for opportunities. People are drawn to your optimism, confidence, and generosity. Opportunities for career advancement, personal growth, and financial gain seem to appear more easily because you are open to receiving them. This magnetic effect can lead to doors opening in ways you may not have expected.

5. **Increased Resilience**

An abundance mindset allows you to bounce back faster from setbacks. Since you view challenges as part of a larger, expansive journey, you don't get bogged down by temporary defeats. Instead of feeling defeated by failure, you see it as a necessary learning experience that will ultimately propel you forward. This resilience helps you stay on course and keeps you motivated to keep going.

How to Cultivate an Abundance Mindset

Adopting an abundance mindset requires intentional practice and commitment. Here are a few practical steps to help you cultivate this game-changing mindset:

1. **Practice Gratitude Daily**

Start each day by listing things you are grateful for. This helps you shift your focus from what you lack to what you already have. Over time, gratitude will become a natural way of thinking and will reinforce your sense of abundance.

2. **Stop Comparing Yourself to Others**

Comparison is a major trap of the scarcity mindset. Instead of measuring your success against others, focus on your own unique path and achievements. Celebrate the success of others without feeling threatened, knowing that their success does not diminish your own potential.

3. **Embrace Challenges as Opportunities**

When faced with challenges, instead of seeing them as roadblocks, reframe them as opportunities for growth. Ask yourself, *"What can I learn from this? How can I use this experience to improve and move forward?"* This mindset shift will help you view obstacles as stepping stones to greater success.

4. **Surround Yourself with Abundance Thinkers**

The people you surround yourself with have a significant impact on your mindset. Spend time with those who embrace abundance and success. Their energy and positivity will inspire and reinforce your own abundance mindset.

5. **Give Generously**

Whether it's sharing your time, resources, or knowledge, practice generosity. When you give without expectation, you invite more abundance into your life. Remember, the more you give, the more you receive.

Conclusion: The Abundance Mindset Is the Key to Unlocking Limitless Success

Shifting to an abundance mindset is one of the most powerful changes you can make to transform your life. It opens you up to a world of limitless possibilities, greater creativity, and lasting success. By focusing on what's possible, celebrating the success of others, and believing in your own potential, you create an environment where success can thrive. The abundance mindset doesn't just change your thoughts; it changes the way you experience the world. It is the key to unlocking a life of fulfilment, growth, and limitless success.

How Abundance Thinking Transforms Your Life

Abundance thinking isn't just a shift in mindset—it's a complete transformation of how you experience the world and interact with it. When you embrace the belief that there is more than enough for everyone, you start to live with a sense of possibility, confidence, and fulfilment. Abundance thinking shifts you from a state of fear and limitation to one of empowerment, growth, and opportunity. This shift has profound impacts on every area of your life, creating positive changes that can last a lifetime.

1. It Increases Your Confidence

One of the most powerful ways that abundance thinking transforms your life is by **boosting your confidence**. When you believe there is enough success, wealth, love, and opportunity to go around, you stop fearing that others' achievements will diminish your own potential. This mindset frees you from the shackles of self-doubt and comparison, allowing you to step into your own power. You begin to trust in your ability to create the life you desire, knowing that the universe has infinite resources and possibilities waiting for you.

With this new confidence, you take bold action toward your goals, knowing that success isn't just a rare chance—it's something that is available to everyone, including you. The belief in abundance propels you forward, helping you to overcome fear and take risks that you otherwise might avoid. Confidence becomes a natural byproduct of living with an abundance mindset.

2. It Opens Doors to Opportunities

When you operate from a mindset of abundance, you begin to see **opportunities everywhere**. Instead of viewing challenges as insurmountable obstacles, you see them as stepping stones to growth. This shift allows you to be more open to new experiences, explore uncharted paths, and take risks without fear of failure.

Abundance thinking encourages you to see potential in situations that others may overlook. It helps you recognize opportunities where others might see scarcity or lack. You start to view the world as full of possibilities, not limitations, and this fresh perspective helps you seize opportunities that align with your true desires.

Whether it's career advancements, personal growth, or new relationships, abundance thinking helps you to remain open, engaged, and active in creating the opportunities you want. Your life begins to reflect this shift, with doors opening that you may have previously thought were closed forever.

3. It Strengthens Relationships

Abundance thinking profoundly impacts your relationships. When you operate from a place of abundance, you stop viewing people as competitors or threats. Instead, you see them as allies, collaborators, and sources of mutual support. The scarcity mindset often breeds envy, jealousy, and rivalry, but abundance thinking promotes **compassion, cooperation, and generosity**.

This shift in perspective fosters deeper, more meaningful connections. You begin to celebrate the successes of others without feeling threatened, knowing that their achievements don't diminish your own potential. You also become more generous with your time, resources, and knowledge, which naturally attracts more positive, supportive people into your life.

In relationships, an abundance mindset means that you trust in the idea that love, respect, and kindness are limitless. You don't worry about "losing" love or attention because you understand that there is always more to give and receive. This sense of connection and shared success strengthens your bonds with others, leading to healthier, more rewarding relationships.

4. It Cultivates a Sense of Gratitude

When you adopt abundance thinking, you begin to cultivate **gratitude** in your daily life. Instead of focusing on what's missing or lacking, you focus on what's already here. You recognize the wealth you already possess—not just in terms of material possessions, but in the love, experiences, health, and opportunities you have.

Gratitude becomes a foundational practice that shapes your perception of the world. It shifts your attention to the present moment, allowing you to appreciate the richness of your life as it is. The more grateful you become, the more you begin to notice and attract positive experiences, people, and opportunities. This cycle of gratitude and abundance fuels itself, creating a ripple effect of positivity in all aspects of your life.

5. It Fosters Personal Growth and Learning

Abundance thinking encourages a **growth-oriented mindset**. Instead of viewing failure or challenges as signs of limitation, you see them as opportunities to learn, improve, and evolve. You begin to understand that every experience—whether good or bad—is a lesson that propels you toward greater success.

With an abundance mindset, you are more likely to seek out new experiences, develop new skills, and challenge yourself in ways that you wouldn't if you were stuck in a scarcity mentality. Abundance thinking frees you from the fear of making mistakes or facing setbacks because you know that growth comes from embracing those moments and learning from them.

This commitment to personal growth leads to a life filled with continuous improvement, self-discovery, and fulfilment. You're no longer afraid to try new things, start new projects, or follow new passions, because you trust in your ability to learn and grow, no matter what happens.

6. It Enhances Your Overall Well-Being

At its core, abundance thinking promotes a sense of **well-being**—both emotionally and physically. When you let go of fear, competition, and lack, you free yourself from stress, anxiety, and overwhelm. The constant pressure of trying to "get ahead" or "keep up" dissipates, leaving room for inner peace and contentment.

Living with an abundance mindset means you are less likely to succumb to the negativity and stress that often accompany scarcity thinking. You feel empowered, in control of your own destiny, and supported by the belief that the world is full of possibilities for you. This mindset fosters a sense of joy, fulfilment, and inner peace, helping you experience life more fully and with a sense of purpose.

7. It Attracts More Abundance into Your Life

Perhaps the most powerful transformation that occurs when you embrace abundance thinking is the ability to **attract more abundance** into your life. The law of attraction tells us that we attract what we focus on. When you focus on abundance—on what you have, on what's possible, and on the opportunities available to you—you naturally begin to draw more of it into your life.

This doesn't mean that everything will magically fall into place, but it does mean that your energy, your mindset, and your actions are aligned with the flow of abundance. You become a magnet for success, opportunities, love, and prosperity because you are living from a place of openness, gratitude, and possibility.

Conclusion: Abundance Thinking Changes Everything

Shifting to an abundance mindset transforms not just your thoughts, but your entire reality. It opens up new possibilities, strengthens your relationships, enhances your well-being, and fosters an environment of growth and opportunity. When you choose to believe in abundance, you shift from a mindset of limitation to one of limitless potential. This mindset allows you to live with greater confidence, resilience, and fulfilment, ultimately creating a life that is not just successful but rich in joy, gratitude, and possibility.

Reprogramming Your Thoughts for Possibilities

Our thoughts are incredibly powerful—they shape our reality, influence our actions, and determine the outcomes we experience. When we focus on limitations and obstacles, our lives often reflect those thoughts. However, when we shift our thinking to embrace possibilities, the world around us begins to open up in exciting and unexpected ways. Reprogramming your thoughts for possibilities isn't about ignoring challenges or pretending everything is perfect— it's about adopting a mindset that actively seeks opportunity, growth, and positive change.

Understanding the Power of Thought

The thoughts you consistently have create the beliefs you hold about yourself, others, and the world. These beliefs form the foundation of your actions and decisions. If you believe that success is out of your reach, that opportunities are limited, or that challenges are insurmountable, those beliefs will influence every aspect of your life, often keeping you stuck in patterns of fear, doubt, and inertia.

On the other hand, when you shift your focus toward possibility, your thoughts become more aligned with creativity, confidence, and optimism. The possibilities you see in the world reflect the possibilities you see within yourself. By reprogramming your thoughts, you unlock the door to a future filled with greater success, personal growth, and happiness.

Step 1: Become Aware of Limiting Beliefs

The first step in reprogramming your thoughts is to become aware of the limiting beliefs you've been holding. These beliefs often come from past experiences, societal conditioning, or fears of failure. Common limiting beliefs include thoughts like:

- "I'm not smart enough to succeed."

- "There's not enough time to achieve my goals."

- "I'll never be able to afford what I want."

- "I'm not worthy of success or happiness."

These thoughts keep you trapped in a cycle of limitation, reinforcing a narrative of lack and scarcity. To reprogram your mind, you first need to acknowledge these beliefs and recognize how they've been influencing your life.

Awareness is the key to breaking free from the grip of these limiting beliefs. Once you realize how often you are thinking in terms of what you can't do, what you lack, or what's impossible, you can begin to intentionally shift your mindset.

Step 2: Challenge and Reframe Negative Thoughts

The next step is to challenge your limiting beliefs and reframe them. Reframing is a powerful technique that allows you to look at a situation from a new perspective. Instead of thinking about what you can't do, ask yourself, "What's possible here?" or "How can I turn this challenge into an opportunity?"

For example, if you're thinking, "I'll never have enough money to start my own business," reframe it by asking, "What are some creative ways I can generate the resources I need to start my business?" This question opens up the possibility of brainstorming new ideas, seeking advice, or finding resources you hadn't previously considered.

Reframing is about creating new mental pathways that focus on what you can do, rather than what you can't. It's about shifting your energy from a place of lack to a place of creative possibility.

Step 3: Replace Limiting Thoughts with Empowering Affirmations

One of the most effective ways to reprogram your mind for possibilities is by using positive affirmations. Affirmations are simple, powerful statements that help replace negative self-talk with empowering thoughts that encourage growth and action. For example:

- Instead of thinking, "I can't achieve my goals," replace it with, "I am capable of creating the success I desire."

- Instead of thinking, "I will never have enough money," reframe it to, "I am open to abundant opportunities and financial growth."

- Instead of thinking, "I don't have the skills," replace it with, "I am constantly learning and growing, and I have the ability to achieve my dreams."

Affirmations work because they help create new neural pathways in your brain. The more you repeat them, the more they become part of your thought pattern. Over time, affirmations shift your subconscious beliefs and influence your behavior, making you more likely to take actions that align with the possibilities you want to create.

Step 4: Visualize Your Success

Visualization is another powerful tool for reprogramming your thoughts for possibilities. The brain doesn't distinguish between a real experience and one vividly imagined. By visualizing your desired outcomes in detail, you activate the neural circuits that would be involved in achieving those goals. This creates a sense of familiarity and confidence in the process, making it easier to take steps toward success.

Spend time each day imagining yourself successfully achieving your goals. Picture the journey, the obstacles you'll overcome, and the satisfaction you'll feel once you reach your destination. This practice not only increases your belief in what's possible, but it also strengthens your resilience in facing challenges along the way.

Visualization also helps you tap into the power of your imagination, allowing you to explore creative solutions and open yourself up to new opportunities that you might not have considered before.

Step 5: Surround Yourself with Possibility-Minded People

The people you spend time with have a significant impact on your mindset. Surrounding yourself with individuals who encourage growth, believe in the power of possibilities, and are actively working toward their own goals can help shift your perspective.

When you're around others who are thinking big and taking bold action, it can inspire you to do the same. Their energy, ideas, and experiences can introduce you to new ways of thinking and seeing the world. These positive influences can help you stay motivated and focused on your possibilities, rather than on your limitations.

Step 6: Take Consistent Action

While reprogramming your thoughts is a crucial part of creating a life full of possibilities, action is what truly brings those possibilities to life. Taking consistent, purposeful action toward your goals helps you align your energy with your thoughts.

Start small if you need to. Each step forward is a victory and a reminder that possibilities are not just abstract ideas—they are real, tangible outcomes that are available to you when you take action. As you begin to move toward your goals, your confidence grows, and your belief in the possibilities expands. This creates a powerful feedback loop that keeps you moving forward, even in the face of challenges.

Step 7: Practice Patience and Trust the Process

Reprogramming your thoughts for possibilities doesn't happen overnight. It's a continual process of shifting your mindset, challenging your beliefs, and taking action. During this process, it's important to practice patience and trust the journey.

Sometimes, the results may not be immediately visible, but by consistently working toward your goals and keeping your thoughts focused on possibility, you are laying the foundation for future success. Trust that your efforts are creating the opportunities you desire, and know that every step you take brings you closer to your vision.

Conclusion: The Power of Possibility

Reprogramming your thoughts for possibilities is one of the most empowering things you can do for yourself. By shifting from a mindset of limitation to one of opportunity, you unlock the potential for growth, success, and fulfilment in all areas of your life. It's about embracing the idea that anything is possible and that the universe is full of opportunities waiting for you to discover. With awareness, consistent practice, and a willingness to challenge old thought patterns, you can rewire your brain for limitless thinking and begin creating a future that reflects the endless possibilities within you.

Practical Step: Gratitude Practices to Shift from Scarcity to Abundance

---

One of the most effective ways to shift from a scarcity mindset to an abundance mindset is by incorporating **gratitude practices** into your daily life. Gratitude has the power to reframe your thoughts, helping you move from a focus on what's lacking to a celebration of what you already have. By consciously practicing gratitude, you can create a sense of abundance and begin to see the richness in every area of your life—whether in relationships, health, opportunities, or success.

Here are some practical steps you can take to harness the power of gratitude and shift your mindset from scarcity to abundance:

1. Start a Daily Gratitude Journal

One of the simplest and most powerful ways to begin cultivating gratitude is by starting a **gratitude journal**. This practice doesn't require any special tools— just a notebook or a journal app and a few minutes each day. The goal is to focus on the things you are grateful for and write them down.

How to do it:

- Every morning or evening, take 5 to 10 minutes to list at least 3 things you're grateful for that day. They can be big or small—anything that brought you joy or appreciation. This could be a compliment you received, a beautiful sunset, time spent with loved ones, or simply the fact that you have a roof over your head and food to eat.

- As you write, feel the emotion behind the gratitude. Really let yourself sink into the positive feelings associated with those things.

By making this a regular practice, you shift your focus away from what's missing or wrong in your life and instead highlight all the positive aspects, no matter how small. This simple act will gradually rewire your brain to focus on abundance, making you more aware of the richness that already exists in your life.

2. Create a Gratitude Jar

A gratitude jar is a fun and tangible way to track your appreciation for the little things in life. It's a reminder that abundance is not just about the grand milestones but also the daily blessings.

How to do it:

- Find a jar and place it somewhere visible.

- Whenever something happens that you're grateful for, write it on a small piece of paper and drop it into the jar.

- At the end of the week or month, read through the notes. This will not only remind you of the abundance in your life but also help you reflect on how much you have to be thankful for.

The physical act of writing and placing the notes in the jar creates a sense of ritual and mindfulness, reinforcing the mindset that life is full of blessings, even when things feel challenging.

3. Practice Gratitude Before Bed

Before you go to sleep, take a few moments to reflect on the day and express gratitude for the experiences you had. This practice can help you end your day on a positive note, allowing you to shift your focus away from any negative thoughts or stressors. It also trains your mind to naturally focus on the positive aspects of your life, even in the face of difficulties.

How to do it:

- Close your eyes and take a few deep breaths to center yourself.

- Think about the day and identify at least three things you are grateful for.

- As you focus on these, allow the feelings of gratitude to fill your body and mind.

- If your mind starts to wander toward stress or worry, gently bring it back to what you're thankful for.

Gratitude before bed helps reframe your mindset to one of appreciation and positivity, setting you up for a restful night and a mindset shift toward abundance.

4. Express Gratitude to Others

A powerful way to reinforce your abundance mindset is by regularly expressing **gratitude to others**. Whether it's a thank-you note, a kind word, or a thoughtful gesture, expressing your appreciation can strengthen your relationships and help you recognize the abundance in the connections you have.

How to do it:

- Take a few minutes each day or week to express genuine gratitude to someone. This could be a colleague, a friend, a family member, or even a stranger.

- Let them know how their actions, support, or presence in your life has made a difference.

- You can send a message, make a phone call, or even give a small gift as a token of appreciation.

By giving thanks to others, you reinforce the belief that there is always enough to go around. Gratitude in relationships also deepens your connections and opens you up to even more positivity and abundance from those around you.

5. Create a Daily Gratitude Affirmation

Another powerful tool for shifting your mindset to one of abundance is by creating a daily **gratitude affirmation**. Affirmations help to reprogram your thoughts by intentionally focusing on positive and abundant statements.

How to do it:

- Create affirmations that resonate with you and reflect gratitude for what you have in your life. For example:

  o "I am grateful for the abundance that flows into my life every day."

  o "I attract opportunities, love, and joy because I focus on the good."

o   "Every day, I find new things to appreciate and celebrate."

- Say these affirmations aloud or silently each morning, or whenever you need a reminder of the abundance around you.

By consistently affirming gratitude, you align your thoughts with abundance, further rewiring your brain to focus on the positive aspects of your life.

6. Practice Gratitude During Challenging Times

It's easy to be grateful when everything is going well, but true transformation happens when you can find gratitude even during difficult moments. Practicing gratitude during challenging times helps shift your perspective and reminds you that abundance is not just about material wealth, but also about resilience, growth, and learning.

How to do it:

- When faced with a challenge, pause and reflect on what you can be grateful for in the situation.

- For example, if you're facing a difficult work project, you might be grateful for the opportunity to learn new skills or the support of your colleagues.

- Acknowledge that even in tough times, there are always things to appreciate, whether it's your strength, the lessons you're learning, or the resources you have at your disposal.

This practice not only boosts your mood but also helps you see the silver linings and find opportunities for growth in adversity.

7. Shift Your Focus Throughout the Day

Throughout your day, make a conscious effort to **shift your focus** to gratitude, especially in moments when you might feel stressed or overwhelmed. You can use simple triggers to remind yourself to practice gratitude, such as when you're waiting in line, commuting, or taking a break.

How to do it:

- Set a timer on your phone or use a reminder to pause and think of something you're grateful for throughout the day.

- As you go about your routine, take a few seconds to appreciate the small moments: the sunshine, a good conversation, the warmth of your coffee, or the comfort of your home.

By integrating gratitude into the small moments of your day, you continuously shift your mindset to one of abundance, helping you see that life is full of positive experiences.

Conclusion: Gratitude as a Gateway to Abundance

Gratitude practices are a simple yet powerful way to shift your mindset from scarcity to abundance. By focusing on the positive aspects of your life, you begin to retrain your brain to seek out possibilities, opportunities, and growth, even in the face of challenges. Whether through journaling, affirmations, or expressing gratitude to others, these practices create a foundation of appreciation that fosters a mindset of abundance. The more you practice gratitude, the more you will begin to see abundance in every area of your life, transforming your perspective and helping you live with greater joy, fulfilment, and success.

8

Cultivating Positivity and Empowerment

The Role of Self-Talk in Creating Your Reality

Your inner dialogue—the conversations you have with yourself on a daily basis—has an immense power to shape your reality. In fact, **self-talk is one of the most influential forces in determining how you perceive yourself, your circumstances, and your future**. It can either uplift you, pushing you toward your dreams, or it can hold you back, reinforcing fear, self-doubt, and limitations. By becoming aware of the power of self-talk, you gain the ability to consciously choose thoughts that empower you, aligning your mindset with the reality you want to create.

What is Self-Talk?

Self-talk refers to the internal dialogue you have in your mind throughout the day. It's the voice that comments on your actions, thoughts, and experiences. Self-talk can be positive, neutral, or negative. Positive self-talk is empowering and encouraging, while negative self-talk often focuses on limitations, failures, or worst-case scenarios.

While self-talk is an ongoing process, the truth is that many of us are unaware of the constant stream of thoughts running through our minds. And yet, whether we're conscious of it or not, those thoughts are impacting how we experience life.

How Self-Talk Shapes Your Reality

Your thoughts are not just passive reflections of reality—they actively **create** your reality. When you repeatedly tell yourself you're not good enough, capable, or deserving, you begin to believe it. These beliefs inform your actions, and the choices you make reflect what you believe is possible for you. On the flip side, when you practice positive self-talk, you begin to change your perceptions of yourself and your potential, which in turn shapes the outcomes in your life.

For example, imagine you are preparing for an important job interview. If your self-talk is dominated by thoughts like, "I'm not qualified enough," "I'm going to mess up," or "They'll never hire me," you'll likely go into the interview feeling anxious, underprepared, and lacking confidence. This mental state may result in behaviors like poor body language, nervousness, or even stumbling over your words—ultimately affecting the outcome.

On the other hand, if your self-talk is positive and empowering, such as, "I've prepared for this," "I am capable of succeeding," or "I have valuable skills to offer," you'll approach the interview with greater confidence and a sense of calm. Your actions will likely reflect this, allowing you to perform at your best and increase the chances of success.

Your inner voice essentially serves as the **filter** through which you view and experience the world. Positive, empowering self-talk opens your mind to opportunities, growth, and success, while negative self-talk keeps you stuck in fear, self-doubt, and limitation.

The Science Behind Self-Talk

Neuroscience has shown that our thoughts have a direct impact on the brain. When we engage in positive self-talk, we stimulate neural pathways that reinforce positive beliefs about ourselves and our potential. In contrast, negative self-talk activates neural circuits that reinforce feelings of inadequacy and fear.

This means that the more we practice positive self-talk, the more we strengthen the neural pathways that support our confidence and ability to succeed. Over time, these pathways become stronger, making it easier to think positively and take empowered actions.

On the other hand, negative self-talk creates a cycle of self-sabotage. The more you feed your mind with limiting beliefs, the more you solidify those beliefs as truths, further reinforcing the cycle of negativity. The good news is that by practicing mindful and intentional self-talk, we can **rewire our brains** to think in ways that support our growth and success.

The Impact of Self-Talk on Self-Worth

One of the most profound ways that self-talk shapes your reality is in its influence on your **self-worth**. When your inner voice is filled with self-criticism, judgment, or doubt, it reinforces feelings of unworthiness. These negative beliefs about yourself create a barrier to personal growth, success, and happiness. You may find yourself avoiding opportunities or holding back from pursuing your goals because you don't believe you deserve them.

On the other hand, when you practice self-compassion and engage in positive self-talk, you begin to build a sense of self-worth that is unshakable. Instead of focusing on your flaws or mistakes, you focus on your strengths, growth, and potential. This empowered sense of self-worth becomes the foundation for taking bold actions and stepping into your full potential.

How to Shift Your Self-Talk

Transforming your self-talk is a gradual process, but it is entirely within your control. Here are some actionable steps to help you shift your inner dialogue and start creating a reality that aligns with your goals and aspirations:

1.   Become Aware of Your Self-Talk

The first step in shifting your self-talk is to become aware of what you're saying to yourself. Pay attention to the language and tone of your inner dialogue. Do you tend to be harsh and critical, or are you encouraging and supportive? Recognize when your self-talk is negative or limiting, and understand how it is influencing your behavior and mindset.

2. Challenge Negative Thoughts

Once you become aware of your negative self-talk, challenge it. Ask yourself, "Is this thought true? Is it helping me move forward?" Often, negative thoughts are exaggerated or not based on facts. By questioning these thoughts, you can begin to replace them with more realistic and empowering beliefs.

For example, if you think, "I'll never be able to do this," challenge that by asking yourself, "What makes me think I can't do this? What skills or strengths do I have that can help me succeed?"

3. Reframe Negative Thoughts into Positive Ones

Reframing is a powerful tool for transforming negative self-talk into positive self-talk. Take a negative thought and turn it into a statement that empowers you. For instance, instead of thinking, "I'm terrible at this," reframe it to, "I'm still learning, but I have the ability to improve." Instead of saying, "I'm not good enough for this opportunity," try thinking, "I am worthy of this opportunity and will grow through the experience."

4. Use Affirmations to Reinforce Positive Beliefs

Affirmations are a powerful tool to shift your self-talk. These are positive statements that you repeat to yourself to help rewire your thinking. For example:

- "I am capable of achieving my goals."

- "I trust myself and my abilities."

- "I deserve success and happiness."

- "I am enough just as I am."

Repeat these affirmations daily to reinforce empowering beliefs about yourself and your potential. Over time, these affirmations will replace negative thoughts with a mindset of confidence and possibility.

5. Be Kind to Yourself

Remember that self-talk is a reflection of how you treat yourself. Be kind, compassionate, and patient with yourself as you shift from self-criticism to self-empowerment. Speak to yourself as you would to a close friend—offering encouragement, understanding, and support. This kindness toward yourself will strengthen your self-worth and boost your confidence.

Conclusion: Empowering Your Reality with Self-Talk

The way you talk to yourself has the power to create the life you desire. Your self-talk can either limit you or propel you forward—it all depends on how you choose to think and speak to yourself. By becoming aware of your inner dialogue and consciously shifting it from negativity to positivity, you can cultivate a mindset that supports growth, confidence, and success. **The stories you tell yourself today shape the reality you live tomorrow.** Strengthening your inner voice is one of the most powerful steps you can take toward creating a life of empowerment and possibility.

How to Recognize and Dismiss Negative Self-Talk

Negative self-talk is often sneaky—it can show up as subtle whispers in your mind or as exaggerated, automatic thoughts that seem completely true in the moment. Over time, these thoughts can shape your self-perception, hinder your confidence, and limit your potential. Recognizing and dismissing negative self-talk is a crucial step in cultivating a mindset of empowerment, positivity, and growth. By learning to identify these thoughts and actively challenge them, you can break free from their grip and begin to create a more empowering inner dialogue.

Step 1: Recognize the Negative Self-Talk Patterns

The first step in dismissing negative self-talk is recognizing when it's happening. Since many of us are used to these negative thoughts, they can easily go unnoticed or become accepted as truth. However, by becoming aware of your internal dialogue, you can begin to catch yourself in the act of thinking negatively.

Signs of Negative Self-Talk:

- **All-or-Nothing Thinking:** You see situations as either completely good or completely bad. For example, "If I make one mistake, I've failed."

- **Overgeneralization:** You take one negative experience and apply it to all situations. For instance, "I didn't get that job, so I'll never succeed."

- **Self-Criticism:** You berate yourself for small mistakes or flaws. For example, "I'm so stupid for messing that up."

- **Catastrophizing:** You imagine the worst-case scenario, even when it's highly unlikely. For example, "If I speak up in the meeting, I'll embarrass myself and lose my job."

- **Labelling:** You assign negative labels to yourself. For instance, "I'm a failure," or "I'm not good enough."

- **Comparing Yourself to Others:** You constantly measure your worth based on how you think others perceive you or how you measure up to them.

If you notice these patterns in your thoughts, it's a sign that you're engaging in negative self-talk. The key is to identify these patterns as they arise, so you can interrupt them before they become ingrained habits.

Step 2: Challenge the Negative Thought

Once you recognize negative self-talk, the next step is to challenge it. Ask yourself if the thought is truly accurate, helpful, or fair. Often, negative self-talk is based on distorted thinking or irrational fears that don't reflect reality.

Questions to Challenge Negative Self-Talk:

- **Is this thought true?** Often, we exaggerate or catastrophize situations in our minds. Ask yourself if the thought is grounded in fact or if it's an overreaction.

- **What evidence do I have to support this thought?** Negative thoughts are rarely backed by solid evidence. Try to counter the thought with facts that support a more positive or realistic perspective.

- **Is there another way to look at this situation?** Reframe the thought by considering a more positive or constructive interpretation of the situation. Instead of "I failed," try thinking, "I learned something valuable that will help me next time."

- **How would I respond if a friend said this about themselves?** This is a great way to put your thoughts in perspective. You'd likely offer your friend kindness and encouragement, so why not do the same for yourself?

By questioning and challenging the validity of your negative thoughts, you create a space for more balanced, rational thinking. Often, you'll realize that the negative self-talk was a product of fear or insecurity, not a true reflection of reality.

Step 3: Reframe and Replace Negative Thoughts

Once you've challenged the negative thought, the next step is to replace it with a more empowering, positive thought. Reframing is a powerful technique that allows you to shift your perspective and change the way you see a situation.

How to Reframe Negative Thoughts:

- **Turn negative thoughts into positive affirmations:** For example, if you catch yourself thinking, "I'm terrible at this," replace it with, "I'm capable of learning and improving."

- **Focus on what you can control:** Instead of saying, "I'll never succeed," reframe it to, "I can take steps to improve and grow."

- **Be specific and kind to yourself:** Instead of vague, harsh statements like, "I'm a failure," reframe it with specifics: "I made a mistake, but that doesn't define me. I can learn from this and do better next time."

- **Use empowering language:** Shift from "I can't" to "I can" or "I'll try." Changing the language you use internally makes a huge difference in how you perceive your ability to succeed.

Reframing negative self-talk isn't about being unrealistic or denying challenges; it's about adopting a more constructive and compassionate perspective. This allows you to face obstacles with confidence, rather than fear and self-doubt.

Step 4: Practice Self-Compassion

Many people struggle with negative self-talk because they are too hard on themselves. They may have high expectations or feel that they need to be perfect in every area of their life. To combat this, practicing **self-compassion** is essential. Being kind to yourself—especially when you make mistakes—helps to reduce the intensity of negative self-talk and fosters a more nurturing inner dialogue.

How to Practice Self-Compassion:

- **Acknowledge your feelings:** Instead of ignoring or suppressing negative emotions, acknowledge them without judgment. Say to yourself, "I'm feeling upset right now, and that's okay."

- **Speak to yourself with kindness:** Treat yourself the same way you would treat a close friend who's going through a tough time. Offer words of encouragement and reassurance.

- **Forgive yourself for mistakes:** Understand that mistakes are part of the learning process. Don't beat yourself up over them—use them as opportunities for growth.

Self-compassion allows you to respond to yourself with understanding, patience, and love, which reduces the power of negative self-talk and builds a foundation for a more positive inner voice.

Step 5: Create New, Positive Self-Talk Habits

Once you've started to recognize and challenge negative self-talk, it's important to replace it with more positive, empowering habits. The more you practice replacing negativity with positivity, the easier it becomes to create lasting change.

Ways to Build Positive Self-Talk Habits:

- **Use positive affirmations regularly:** Affirmations are a powerful way to rewire your brain to think more positively. Choose affirmations that resonate with your goals, strengths, and aspirations. Repeat them daily to reinforce empowering beliefs.

- **Surround yourself with positive influences:** The people you spend time with, the media you consume, and the environments you expose yourself to all influence your self-talk. Choose to engage with uplifting, supportive, and positive people and content.

- **Celebrate small victories:** Recognize and celebrate your accomplishments, no matter how small. Acknowledging your progress helps build confidence and reinforces positive self-talk.

- **Practice mindfulness:** Mindfulness helps you become more aware of your thoughts and emotions, allowing you to catch negative self-talk as it arises. By staying present and non-judgmental, you can interrupt negative thought patterns and redirect your focus to more positive ones.

Conclusion: Letting Go of Negative Self-Talk

Negative self-talk may have been a habitual part of your thinking for a long time, but that doesn't mean it's permanent. By recognizing it, challenging it, reframing it, and replacing it with positive, empowering thoughts, you can take control of your inner dialogue and start creating a reality that reflects your true potential. **Your thoughts shape your life**, and by consciously choosing to let go of negativity, you can cultivate a mindset that supports success, self-love, and limitless possibilities.

Harnessing the Power of a Positive Inner Dialogue

Your inner dialogue is the silent yet powerful conversation you have with yourself throughout each day. It shapes how you perceive yourself, your potential, and the world around you. The thoughts you entertain, the words you speak to yourself, and the stories you tell yourself create the lens through which you experience life. Harnessing the power of a positive inner dialogue can be a game-changer in your journey toward personal growth, success, and happiness.

A positive inner dialogue isn't about being unrealistically optimistic or ignoring challenges. Instead, it's about choosing to focus on solutions, possibilities, and growth rather than fear, limitations, and negativity. It's about cultivating a mindset that empowers you to believe in your potential, handle setbacks with resilience, and take action toward your dreams.

The Impact of Positive Inner Dialogue

Positive self-talk can radically change the way you approach life. It influences your thoughts, emotions, behaviors, and even your physical well-being. When your inner dialogue is supportive and encouraging, it boosts your self-confidence, enhances your decision-making, and enables you to face challenges with a sense of empowerment.

Conversely, negative self-talk can undermine your confidence, cloud your judgment, and make even the simplest tasks feel insurmountable. A positive inner dialogue, on the other hand, builds mental strength, fosters emotional resilience, and encourages a mindset of abundance and possibility.

For instance, when faced with an opportunity to speak in public, your inner dialogue might go one of two ways:

- **Negative Self-Talk:** "I'm terrible at speaking in front of people. I'm going to embarrass myself."

- **Positive Self-Talk:** "I've prepared for this. I'm capable, and I have valuable insights to share."

Notice how the second example invites confidence, calm, and a belief in your abilities, whereas the first example brings in anxiety and self-doubt. The power of your thoughts can be the difference between success and failure, fear and courage, or growth and stagnation.

How Positive Self-Talk Rewires Your Brain

One of the most fascinating aspects of positive self-talk is its ability to physically reshape your brain. The brain is not a static organ; it has the incredible ability to change and adapt—this phenomenon is known as **neuroplasticity**. When you engage in positive thinking and practice positive self-talk, you are essentially rewiring your brain to strengthen pathways that support confidence, optimism, and success.

Research has shown that repeated positive self-talk can lead to increased brain activity in areas related to motivation, emotional regulation, and goal achievement. As you practice focusing on empowering thoughts, you're encouraging the brain to form new connections that support positive outcomes. Over time, positive thinking becomes a habit—an automatic response to situations, rather than something you have to consciously force.

Practical Strategies for Cultivating Positive Inner Dialogue

1. Replace Negative Thoughts with Positive Affirmations

Affirmations are short, positive statements that you repeat to yourself to reprogram your subconscious mind. For example:

- "I am capable of achieving my goals."

- "I trust myself and my abilities."

- "I handle challenges with grace and resilience."

By repeating these affirmations daily, you shift your internal narrative and begin to replace limiting beliefs with empowering ones. When negative thoughts arise, consciously replace them with affirmations that reflect your strengths and potential. Over time, affirmations become deeply ingrained in your thought process, making positive self-talk your default mindset.

2. Practice Gratitude Daily

Gratitude is a powerful tool for fostering a positive inner dialogue. By focusing on what you're thankful for—whether it's small moments of joy or major accomplishments—you shift your attention away from what's wrong or lacking in your life to what's abundant and good. This mindset shift opens the door to more positivity, helping you create a mental environment where success and possibility thrive.

Consider starting each day by listing three things you're grateful for. This simple practice can dramatically improve your overall outlook and foster a sense of optimism, which directly influences the way you talk to yourself. Gratitude reinforces the belief that there's always something positive to focus on, even in challenging times.

3. Use Visualization to Reinforce Positive Beliefs

Visualization is a powerful technique used by top performers to enhance confidence and success. When you visualize a positive outcome, you're engaging in a mental rehearsal that helps your brain prepare for success. Combine visualization with positive self-talk by imagining yourself succeeding and speaking to yourself in encouraging, affirming ways during the visualization process.

For example, if you're preparing for a big presentation, close your eyes and picture yourself delivering your talk confidently. As you visualize the scene, repeat affirmations such as, "I am calm, confident, and prepared. I communicate clearly and effectively." This combination of imagery and positive self-talk primes your brain for success and boosts your self-esteem.

4. Be Mindful of the Language You Use

Language is incredibly powerful. The words you use, both internally and externally, shape your experience. Pay close attention to the language of your inner dialogue. Are you using words like "can't," "never," or "always"? These words are often indicators of negative or limiting thoughts. Instead, replace them with more empowering language, such as "I can," "I'm learning," or "I choose." Small shifts in your language can have a profound impact on the way you view yourself and your abilities.

5. Surround Yourself with Positive Influences

Your inner dialogue is also influenced by the people and environments around you. Surround yourself with individuals who uplift and encourage you. Engage with positive content—whether it's books, podcasts, or social media—that reinforces empowering messages and supports your personal growth. When you immerse yourself in positivity, it becomes easier to cultivate a positive inner dialogue.

The Ripple Effect of Positive Inner Dialogue

When you begin to harness the power of a positive inner dialogue, the benefits ripple outward into every area of your life. Your relationships improve because you become more confident and secure in yourself. You approach challenges with resilience and creativity because you believe in your ability to handle adversity. Your work and personal projects flourish because you take bold, empowered action, trusting that you have what it takes to succeed.

A positive inner dialogue doesn't just change the way you think—it transforms the way you show up in the world. It encourages you to take risks, embrace failure as a stepping stone, and persist in the face of obstacles. With every positive thought you think, you are reinforcing your belief in yourself and your potential.

Conclusion: The Power is in Your Words

Your inner dialogue is one of the most powerful tools you have in creating the life you want. By consciously shifting your self-talk from negativity to positivity, you are rewiring your brain, strengthening your confidence, and empowering yourself to take bold actions. The more you practice positive inner dialogue, the more you'll experience the incredible impact it can have on your success, happiness, and overall sense of well-being. **You are the author of your story, and the words you speak to yourself today will shape the reality you live tomorrow.** Harness the power of your positive inner dialogue and step into a life of limitless possibilities.

Creating Empowering Beliefs for Long-Term Success

Your beliefs shape every aspect of your life. They are the lenses through which you view the world, influencing your actions, decisions, and the opportunities you pursue. While some beliefs are formed by experiences and external influences, you have the power to create new, empowering beliefs that serve your long-term success and well-being. By intentionally choosing beliefs that align with your vision, values, and goals, you can unlock your full potential and create lasting change in your life.

Empowering beliefs are thoughts and convictions that empower you to take action, persist in the face of adversity, and see challenges as opportunities for growth. These beliefs help you trust in your abilities, recognize your worth, and approach life with a mindset of abundance and possibility. When you cultivate empowering beliefs, you build the mental foundation for long-term success—whether in your personal life, career, relationships, or health.

Understanding the Power of Beliefs

Beliefs are not just abstract ideas—they are the subconscious rules you live by. They influence your thoughts, feelings, and behaviors without you even realizing it. For example, if you believe that "success is hard to achieve" or "I'm not good enough to reach my goals," your actions will reflect those limiting beliefs. You may hesitate to take risks, avoid pursuing opportunities, or quit before you give yourself a fair chance to succeed.

On the other hand, if you cultivate beliefs such as "I am capable of achieving anything I set my mind to" or "Challenges are simply opportunities for growth," you will act in ways that align with these empowering beliefs. You'll be more confident in your abilities, more willing to embrace challenges, and more determined to persevere when faced with setbacks.

The beliefs you hold about yourself and the world around you directly impact your outcomes. Empowering beliefs act as catalysts for growth and success, while limiting beliefs hold you back from reaching your true potential.

The Role of Self-Awareness in Shaping Beliefs

Before you can create empowering beliefs, it's essential to first identify the limiting beliefs that may be holding you back. These often stem from past experiences, societal conditioning, or negative self-talk. Common limiting beliefs include:

- "I'm not worthy of success."

- "I'm too old/young to start something new."

- "I always fail, so why try?"

- "I'm not as smart or talented as others."

Once you recognize these limiting beliefs, you can begin to challenge and reframe them. Acknowledging them is the first step in transforming them into empowering beliefs that support your growth.

How to Create Empowering Beliefs for Long-Term Success

1. Identify and Challenge Limiting Beliefs

The first step in creating empowering beliefs is to become aware of the negative or limiting beliefs you hold. These beliefs often manifest as internal dialogue that holds you back. For example, if you catch yourself thinking, "I'm not good enough to achieve my goals," take a moment to challenge this belief. Ask yourself questions like:

- **Is this belief really true?**

- **What evidence do I have that contradicts this belief?**

- **How would I approach life if I didn't hold this belief?**

By questioning the validity of your limiting beliefs, you start to break their hold over you. Recognize that beliefs are not facts—they are thoughts you've accepted as truth. Once you realize this, you can shift your focus to more empowering perspectives.

2. Reframe Limiting Beliefs into Empowering Ones

Once you've identified your limiting beliefs, the next step is to reframe them into positive, empowering beliefs. For example:

- **Limiting Belief:** "I'm not good enough to succeed."

- **Empowering Belief:** "I have the skills, determination, and ability to succeed, and I'm always learning and growing."

Reframing is a powerful tool because it allows you to shift your focus from what's holding you back to what's possible. When you reframe your thoughts, you change your perception of yourself and your potential. You shift from a mindset of limitation to one of possibility and growth.

3. Create New Beliefs That Align with Your Vision

Empowering beliefs are most effective when they are aligned with your goals and aspirations. Reflect on the future you want to create and the person you want to become. What beliefs would support that version of yourself? For example:

- "I am worthy of success and abundance."

- "Every challenge is an opportunity to learn and grow."

- "I am capable of achieving anything I set my mind to."

Write these beliefs down and commit to repeating them regularly. The more you focus on these positive, empowering beliefs, the more they will become ingrained in your subconscious mind. Over time, these beliefs will shape your actions and outcomes.

4. Use Affirmations to Reinforce Empowering Beliefs

Affirmations are a powerful tool for reinforcing new beliefs. By repeating affirmations daily, you reprogram your subconscious mind to accept empowering thoughts as truth. Choose affirmations that reflect your desired outcomes, such as:

- "I am confident, capable, and unstoppable."

- "I have all the resources I need to succeed."

- "I embrace challenges as opportunities to grow and improve."

Say these affirmations out loud, write them down, or even record them and listen to them regularly. The more consistently you reinforce these positive beliefs, the more they will shape your mindset and your life.

5. Visualize Your Success

Visualization is another powerful technique to reinforce empowering beliefs. When you visualize yourself achieving your goals, you activate the areas of your brain associated with success, motivation, and achievement. Visualizing your success strengthens your belief in your ability to make it a reality.

Spend time each day visualizing yourself living your dream life, whether it's in your career, relationships, or health. See yourself overcoming obstacles, making progress, and celebrating your achievements. During these visualizations, repeat your empowering beliefs to further solidify them in your mind.

6. Surround Yourself with Positive Influences

Your beliefs are influenced not only by your inner dialogue but also by the people and environments you surround yourself with. If you want to cultivate empowering beliefs, it's essential to be around people who encourage, support, and believe in you. Seek out mentors, friends, and communities that uplift you and help you grow.

Additionally, consume content—books, podcasts, videos—that inspires and motivates you. The more positive influences you expose yourself to, the easier it becomes to adopt empowering beliefs that align with your success.

The Long-Term Benefits of Empowering Beliefs

Creating empowering beliefs is not just about achieving short-term goals—it's about building a foundation for long-term success. Empowering beliefs lead to greater self-confidence, resilience, and the ability to handle life's challenges with grace. They encourage you to take action, learn from your mistakes, and keep moving forward, even in the face of adversity.

When you believe in yourself and your potential, you are more likely to take risks, embrace new opportunities, and push past fear and doubt. Empowering beliefs fuel your persistence and perseverance, which are key ingredients for long-term success. As you continue to reinforce these beliefs, they will become the driving force behind your achievements, growth, and personal transformation.

Conclusion: Empower Your Mindset for Unlimited Success

The beliefs you hold about yourself and your capabilities are the foundation of your success. By intentionally creating empowering beliefs that align with your goals, values, and vision for the future, you can transform your mindset and unlock your full potential. Remember, beliefs are not set in stone—they are dynamic and can be reshaped at any time. Take control of your thoughts, rewrite the narrative that no longer serves you, and create a belief system that empowers you to achieve long-term success. When you believe in your greatness, you open the door to limitless possibilities.

Practical Step: Daily Positive Affirmations and Visualization Techniques

One of the most powerful tools you can use to transform your mindset, boost your confidence, and unlock your potential is the daily practice of **positive affirmations** and **visualization techniques**. These practices are simple yet profoundly effective in shifting your thoughts, reprogramming your subconscious, and creating a reality that aligns with your highest goals and desires.

Both affirmations and visualization work together to help you reinforce empowering beliefs, reduce self-doubt, and move toward your dreams with a sense of certainty and optimism. By integrating these practices into your daily routine, you will strengthen your inner resolve, boost your self-worth, and align your actions with your deepest aspirations.

What Are Positive Affirmations?

Positive affirmations are short, powerful statements that reflect your desired reality and reinforce positive beliefs about yourself, your abilities, and your life. They are the antidote to negative self-talk and limiting beliefs. When you repeat affirmations consistently, you begin to change your thought patterns and shift your mindset toward empowerment and possibility.

For example:

- "I am worthy of love, success, and happiness."
- "I have the power to create the life I desire."
- "Every challenge I face is an opportunity to grow."
- "I am capable, confident, and unstoppable."

The key to making affirmations effective is to make them specific, present tense, and personal. Instead of saying, "I will be successful," say, "I am successful, and I am taking steps toward my goals every day." This shifts your focus from a future event to the present moment, allowing you to act as if the success is already happening.

How to Use Affirmations Effectively

1. **Consistency is Key:** The more frequently you practice affirmations, the more they will sink into your subconscious mind. Aim to repeat your affirmations multiple times a day—ideally in the morning to start your day on a positive note and before bed to reinforce your beliefs as you drift into sleep.

2. **Speak with Conviction:** When you say your affirmations, say them with emotion and belief. The more conviction you put behind your words, the more powerful the impact. Stand tall, speak clearly, and imagine yourself already embodying the affirmation.

3. **Write Them Down:** Writing your affirmations down further solidifies them in your mind. You can keep a journal where you write your affirmations each day or write them on sticky notes and place them where you'll see them regularly—like on your mirror, desk, or in your car. This constant exposure will keep your focus aligned with your positive beliefs.

What is Visualization?

Visualization is the practice of mentally imagining yourself achieving your goals and living your desired life. It is a creative and transformative technique that harnesses the power of the mind to create a vivid image of success, fulfilment, and abundance. Just as athletes use visualization to mentally rehearse their performance, you can use it to mentally rehearse your success.

When you visualize, you are essentially telling your brain that your goals are possible, and you begin to cultivate the emotions and mindset necessary to bring them to life. Visualization helps you feel the feelings of success, which in turn motivates you to take inspired action toward your goals.

How to Use Visualization Effectively

1. **Get into a Relaxed State:** Find a quiet, comfortable place where you can close your eyes and relax. Take a few deep breaths to calm your mind and body. The more relaxed you are, the more vivid and effective your visualizations will be.

2. **Be Specific and Detailed:** The more detailed and specific you can make your visualization, the more powerful it will be. Imagine every sensory detail—how you look, how you feel, what you hear, and even the smells or sensations. For example, if you're visualizing a successful

presentation, picture yourself standing confidently in front of an audience, speaking clearly, and feeling energized. Imagine the positive feedback, the applause, and the sense of accomplishment you'll experience.

3. **Visualize Daily:** Just like affirmations, visualization is most effective when practiced consistently. Set aside time each day—ideally in the morning or before bed—to spend a few minutes visualizing your success. The more frequently you visualize, the more your brain will begin to see it as a reality.

4. **Feel the Emotions:** One of the most important aspects of visualization is the emotional experience. When you visualize success, allow yourself to feel the emotions associated with achieving your goals—whether that's excitement, pride, gratitude, or joy. These emotions strengthen your belief in your goals and activate the areas of your brain responsible for motivation and action.

5. **Combine Visualization with Affirmations:** For an even more powerful practice, combine your affirmations with visualization. As you visualize yourself succeeding, repeat your empowering affirmations. For example, as you imagine achieving your dream job, you might say, "I am worthy of success and I am fully capable of achieving my dreams." This combination reinforces both the mental image and the belief that it's already happening.

Practical Tips for Integration into Your Daily Routine

1. **Morning Routine:** Start your day with positive affirmations to set the tone for success. Stand in front of a mirror, look yourself in the eyes, and repeat your affirmations with belief. Spend a few minutes visualizing your ideal day and how you'll handle challenges with confidence.

2. **Throughout the Day:** Whenever you catch yourself slipping into negative thoughts, use your affirmations to redirect your mindset. You can also take brief moments throughout the day to visualize small successes—whether it's acing a meeting, finishing a project, or having a positive interaction with someone.

3. **Nighttime Practice:** Before going to sleep, spend a few minutes visualizing your long-term goals and repeating your affirmations. The subconscious mind is highly receptive during sleep, so this practice helps to reinforce your empowering beliefs while you rest.

The Power of Consistency

The key to success with both affirmations and visualization is consistency. These techniques are like exercise for your mind; the more regularly you practice, the stronger and more automatic your positive beliefs and thoughts become. Over time, your inner dialogue shifts from one of doubt and fear to one of confidence and possibility. You'll begin to notice changes in your behavior, your actions, and your results.

Conclusion: Harnessing the Power of Your Mind

By making positive affirmations and visualization a daily practice, you are taking control of your thoughts and emotions, setting yourself up for long-term success. These tools help you reprogram your subconscious mind, overcome limiting beliefs, and align your actions with your highest potential. Remember, the power to create the life you desire is within you. Every time you speak words of empowerment and visualize your success, you are building the foundation for the future you want. With patience, practice, and consistency, these techniques will transform the way you think, act, and live.

9

Manifesting Your New Reality – From Dreamer to Doer

Turning Limitless Thinking into Action

L imitless thinking is the foundation of all transformation. It opens the door to new possibilities, removes mental barriers, and encourages you to dream beyond your current reality. But, while limitless thinking creates the vision, action is what brings that vision to life. Without action, even the most inspiring ideas remain just that—ideas.

Turning your limitless thinking into actionable steps is the key to manifesting the life you desire. It's not enough to think big; you must also be willing to take consistent, intentional action toward your goals. When you bridge the gap between vision and execution, you move from being a dreamer to a doer, and that's when true transformation happens.

The Power of Action: Why It's Essential

Action is the bridge between where you are and where you want to be. Even the most positive mindset and powerful thoughts will not bring tangible results unless they are paired with intentional steps forward. The power of action lies in its ability to move you from intention to reality. Each action you take is a physical manifestation of the limitless thinking you've cultivated.

Action fuels momentum. The more you act on your ideas, the more confidence and clarity you gain. As you take consistent steps toward your dreams, you begin to see evidence that your vision is possible, reinforcing your limitless mindset. Action also helps you overcome fear and doubt by proving that you are capable and worthy of success. It moves you away from the realm of theory into the tangible world of results.

Aligning Your Goals with Actionable Steps

One of the most effective ways to turn your limitless thinking into action is to break down your larger goals into smaller, manageable steps. It's easy to feel overwhelmed when you look at your dreams as a whole, but when you focus on the smaller tasks, it becomes much easier to make progress.

Start by clarifying your end goal—what is your ultimate vision? Once you have a clear sense of what you want to achieve, break that goal down into smaller, more specific actions that you can take every day. This way, instead of getting caught up in the enormity of the journey, you're simply focusing on what's in front of you.

For example, if your goal is to write a book, instead of saying, "I'm going to write a book," break it down into steps such as:

- **Write 500 words a day.**

- **Create an outline for the chapters.**

- **Research publishing options.**

By breaking your big goal into smaller, concrete tasks, you eliminate overwhelm and create a roadmap that helps you stay focused on the present moment.

Overcoming Procrastination and Fear of Failure

Procrastination is often the result of fear and perfectionism. You may feel paralyzed by the pressure to get everything right or by the fear of failure. However, limitless thinking is about embracing progress over perfection. When you shift your mindset to believe that every step forward is a success, you'll start to overcome the inertia that holds you back.

To combat procrastination:

1. **Start with Small Wins**: The easiest way to build momentum is by starting small. Commit to just a few minutes of action each day. Whether it's writing one page or making one phone call, small actions compound into big results.

2. **Let Go of Perfectionism**: Accept that mistakes and failures are part of the journey. You don't need to do everything perfectly to move forward. Every step, no matter how imperfect, is progress.

3. **Set Time-Based Goals**: Commit to a certain amount of time for focused work. Setting a timer for 20 or 30 minutes can help you avoid distractions and make the task feel more manageable.

4. **Accountability**: Share your goals with someone you trust or create a public commitment. When someone else knows what you're working toward, it adds an element of accountability that makes you more likely to take consistent action.

The Importance of Consistency and Persistence

Limitless thinking requires consistency. It's easy to get excited about a new idea or project, but maintaining your momentum is where most people struggle. It's essential to take action daily, even if it's just a small step. Consistency is what compounds and builds the momentum necessary to transform your dreams into reality.

Persistence is equally important. There will be setbacks, challenges, and moments of doubt along the way. But with limitless thinking, you reframe these moments as opportunities to learn and grow, not as reasons to quit. By staying persistent in your efforts, you teach yourself to overcome obstacles and keep moving forward, no matter what.

Creating an Action Plan: Turning Dreams Into Doable Steps

To effectively turn limitless thinking into action, create a clear action plan. This plan should outline specific steps, timelines, and measurable milestones that will guide your journey. Here's how to create your own:

1. **Define Your Big Picture Goal**: Write down your ultimate goal. What do you want to manifest in your life? Be as specific as possible—this could be personal, professional, or a combination of both.

2. **Break It Down**: Identify smaller, actionable tasks that will bring you closer to your goal. What specific actions can you take on a daily, weekly, and monthly basis? These tasks should be measurable and achievable.

3. **Set Deadlines**: Give each task a clear deadline. Deadlines create a sense of urgency and help you stay on track. Without deadlines, it's easy to put things off indefinitely.

4. **Prioritize Tasks**: Not all tasks are equally important. Focus on the tasks that will have the biggest impact on your goal first. This helps you avoid getting bogged down by trivial details.

5. **Review and Adjust**: Regularly assess your progress. What's working well? What needs to be adjusted? Sometimes, taking action reveals new insights that help you course-correct along the way.

The Role of Belief in Action

Action becomes effortless when you believe that success is inevitable. Limitless thinking fuels that belief. As you take each step toward your goal, remind yourself that you are worthy of success and that your dreams are within reach. This belief will drive you to continue acting even when things get tough, and it will sustain your momentum long after the initial excitement fades.

Belief is the fuel for action, and action is the vehicle that takes you to your destination. By reinforcing your limitless thinking with positive beliefs and taking consistent action, you set yourself up for success.

Conclusion: From Dreamer to Doer

Turning limitless thinking into action requires a commitment to consistent effort and a belief in your ability to succeed. While the vision and ideas are essential, it's the action that ultimately brings them to life. By breaking down your goals into manageable steps, overcoming procrastination, and staying persistent, you will transform your dreams into reality. Remember, every small action you take brings you one step closer to your ultimate goal. Move from dreaming about what could be to doing what you know is possible. With limitless thinking and consistent action, you will manifest the life you truly desire.

The Art of Goal-Setting with a Limitless Mindset

Goal-setting is a powerful tool for turning your dreams into tangible outcomes, but how you set your goals and the mindset you approach them with can make all the difference. When you approach goal-setting with a **limitless mindset**, you shift the process from one of constraint to one of endless possibility. A limitless mindset invites creativity, flexibility, and the belief that there are no limits to what you can achieve. It empowers you to think bigger, take bold actions, and persist through challenges.

Setting goals with a limitless mindset isn't just about listing objectives; it's about creating a vision for your life that reflects your highest potential and aligns with your deepest values. It requires you to see beyond current limitations—whether they're self-imposed or external—and embrace the endless opportunities that exist when you tap into your full potential.

The Power of a Limitless Mindset in Goal-Setting

When you adopt a limitless mindset in goal-setting, you stop viewing obstacles as barriers and start seeing them as opportunities for growth. This shift in perspective allows you to approach your goals with an unwavering belief that every setback is temporary and every challenge is part of the journey to success.

Here's why a limitless mindset transforms the way you set goals:

1. **Expands Your Vision:** Instead of thinking small or settling for what feels "safe," you allow yourself to dream bigger. You create a vision that excites and motivates you, one that makes you feel inspired and driven to push past fear and self-doubt.

2. **Encourages Bold Action:** When you believe anything is possible, you become more willing to take risks. A limitless mindset fuels the courage to step out of your comfort zone and take action even when the path is unclear. It's about trusting that you will figure things out along the way.

3. **Fosters Resilience:** With a limitless mindset, you embrace failure not as defeat, but as feedback. You understand that setbacks are part of the process, and they don't diminish your ability to achieve your goals. Instead, they strengthen your resilience, helping you develop the perseverance needed to keep going.

4. **Promotes Growth and Adaptability:** A limitless mindset isn't fixed. It encourages flexibility in how you approach your goals. If one path doesn't work, you're open to finding another. You're less attached to the exact outcome and more focused on the lessons learned and progress made.

Steps to Set Goals with a Limitless Mindset

1. Clarify Your Vision

The first step in setting goals with a limitless mindset is to get crystal clear on your vision. What do you truly want to create in your life? When you allow yourself to dream without limitations, you begin to uncover what really excites and motivates you.

Ask yourself:

*   What would I do if I knew I could not fail?

*   What would make me feel most fulfilled?

*   If I could achieve anything in the next year, five years, or ten years, what would that be?

The clearer and more vivid your vision, the more motivation and drive you will have to take action toward it.

2. Set Big, Audacious Goals

Once you have a clear vision, set **big** goals—goals that inspire you, challenge you, and push you beyond your current limits. These goals should feel exciting and a bit uncomfortable. They should make you stretch and grow. The bigger the goal, the more room there is for creativity and growth.

Instead of setting goals that feel safe or small, aim for those that scare you a little, the ones that make you think, "Is this even possible?" That is the energy you want to bring to your goal-setting process—goals that spark excitement and drive.

3. Break Goals Down into Actionable Steps

Even though your goals should be big, breaking them down into smaller, actionable steps is essential. The limitless mindset allows you to dream big without feeling overwhelmed because you know that small steps will lead you to your big vision. Each action you take, no matter how small, is a step closer to your ultimate goal.

For example, if your goal is to launch your own business, break it down into smaller tasks:

- Research business ideas.

- Write a business plan.

- Secure funding.

- Create your website.

- Start marketing.

- Connect with potential customers.

By focusing on individual tasks, you maintain momentum and avoid feeling overwhelmed by the scale of the larger goal.

4. Embrace Flexibility and Adaptability

While it's important to stay focused on your goals, it's equally important to remain flexible in your approach. The limitless mindset reminds you that there's no single "right" way to achieve your dreams. You might face unexpected challenges, and your plans may need to shift along the way. Embrace change and adaptability, knowing that each detour is an opportunity for growth.

If one method doesn't work, try another. If you encounter a roadblock, reassess and adjust your strategy. Flexibility doesn't mean giving up on your goal—it means staying open to new possibilities and creative solutions.

5. Take Bold and Consistent Action

No matter how clear your vision or how audacious your goals, without action, your dreams remain just that—dreams. A limitless mindset propels you into bold, consistent action. You'll move from thinking about what you *could* do to taking the concrete steps to make it happen.

It's about making progress every single day, no matter how small. Celebrate each step forward, and don't get discouraged by setbacks. Remember, consistency compounds, and even the smallest efforts will eventually lead to extraordinary results.

6. Cultivate a Positive and Empowering Belief System

Your beliefs are the foundation of everything you achieve. If you believe that you are capable and worthy of success, you will take the necessary steps to reach your goals. If you believe that success is limited to others, or that you aren't good enough, you will subconsciously sabotage your efforts.

To set goals with a limitless mindset, begin by affirming your worth and your potential. Use positive affirmations and empowering thoughts to counteract any negative self-talk. The more you reinforce your belief in yourself, the more confident you will become in pursuing your big goals.

7. Measure Progress and Celebrate Wins

Lastly, measure your progress along the way and celebrate your wins—big and small. A limitless mindset celebrates growth, not perfection. Every step forward, no matter how small, is evidence of your power and determination.

Tracking your progress not only keeps you motivated, but it also helps you see how far you've come, especially when the journey feels long or difficult. Take time to reflect on your achievements, no matter how minor they may seem, and give yourself credit for the progress you've made.

Conclusion: Your Goals Are Limitless, Too

Setting goals with a limitless mindset isn't just about aiming for the highest level of success—it's about embracing the limitless potential within yourself. When you think without boundaries, your goals become more than just tasks—they become a powerful expression of your vision, values, and aspirations.

By clarifying your vision, setting bold goals, taking consistent action, and embracing adaptability, you turn your dreams into achievable realities. A limitless mindset enables you to break free from constraints, recognize the infinite possibilities before you, and take the steps needed to manifest your dreams. With this mindset, there's nothing stopping you—your goals are within reach, and the journey is just as exciting as the destination.

Aligning Your Actions with Your Higher Purpose

Living with purpose is one of the most fulfilling ways to create a meaningful and transformative life. However, it's not enough to simply have a sense of purpose; aligning your daily actions with that purpose is what truly brings it to life. When your actions are aligned with your higher purpose, every step you take is infused with intention, passion, and fulfilment.

But aligning your actions with your higher purpose isn't always easy. In today's world, we are often pulled in many directions, distracted by external pressures and short-term goals. It's easy to lose sight of what truly matters—what resonates with your soul, what sparks joy, and what brings you a deep sense of fulfilment. That's why it's crucial to consciously align your actions with your higher purpose so that your life is a reflection of your deepest values and aspirations.

Understanding Your Higher Purpose

Your higher purpose is the unique contribution you are here to make in the world. It is tied to your passions, strengths, and values and often goes beyond personal achievement. It's about the impact you want to have—on others, on your community, and on the world.

To clarify your higher purpose, consider the following:

- **What are you passionate about?** The things that light you up often provide clues to your purpose.

- **What comes naturally to you?** Your talents and strengths are often indicators of how you are meant to serve others.

- **What do you want to leave behind?** Think about the legacy you want to create, the difference you want to make in the world.

Once you have clarity on your higher purpose, you'll begin to see how everything else in your life can be shaped around it.

The Power of Purpose-Driven Action

When your actions align with your higher purpose, you move with clarity and conviction. Every decision becomes easier because you know what's in alignment with your purpose and what isn't. Purpose-driven actions fuel passion and motivation—they give you a reason to keep going, even in the face of challenges or setbacks.

Here's why purpose-driven action is so powerful:

1. **It Fuels Motivation**: When your actions align with your higher purpose, you are more motivated to take consistent action. Purpose gives you a "why" that's greater than just achieving a specific goal.

2. **It Brings Fulfilment**: Success achieved without purpose can feel hollow or empty. But when your actions are connected to a deeper sense of meaning, every step, no matter how small, feels significant and fulfilling.

3. **It Creates Alignment in Your Life**: Aligning your actions with your higher purpose brings harmony to your life. You begin to attract opportunities, people, and experiences that resonate with your true self. Your life becomes more synchronized with your values and aspirations.

4. **It Improves Decision-Making**: With purpose as your compass, decision-making becomes much easier. You'll instinctively know which opportunities to pursue and which ones to pass on because they will either be aligned or misaligned with your higher purpose.

Practical Steps to Align Your Actions with Your Higher Purpose

1. Clarify Your Purpose

The first step is gaining clarity on what your higher purpose is. This is a continual process that evolves as you grow. However, start by asking yourself key questions about your passions, strengths, and the kind of impact you want to make in the world. Write down your answers, and refine them over time. Journaling and reflection exercises are great tools for deepening your understanding of your purpose.

2. Set Purpose-Driven Goals

Once you have clarity on your higher purpose, set goals that are aligned with it. Instead of focusing solely on career advancement or material success, consider how your goals contribute to your larger purpose. Ask yourself: *How do these goals serve not only me but also others? How do they reflect my values and passions?*

For example, if your purpose is to inspire and uplift others, you might set a goal to write a book, mentor young people, or start a charitable initiative. If your purpose is centered around creativity, your goal might be to launch an art project that expresses your unique vision of the world.

3. Take Daily Action

Consistency is key to alignment. Taking purposeful, aligned action every day helps you stay connected to your higher purpose. Even small, daily steps— whether it's dedicating time to a creative project, volunteering, or learning something new—will move you closer to your vision.

It's important to note that aligned action doesn't always have to be grand or dramatic. It's the simple, everyday actions that accumulate over time and make a significant difference.

4. Stay Mindful and Present

Living in alignment with your purpose requires mindfulness. By staying present in each moment, you're more likely to notice opportunities that are aligned with your purpose. Being mindful also helps you avoid distractions that might pull you away from your true path. Whether it's through meditation, deep breathing, or simply being more aware of your thoughts and feelings, staying grounded helps you stay connected to your purpose and your actions.

5. Let Go of What's Not Aligned

To align your actions with your higher purpose, you may need to let go of activities, relationships, or commitments that no longer serve you. This can be difficult, especially if you've invested time or energy into something that no longer fits with your goals. However, releasing what is misaligned creates space for what truly matters.

Consider asking yourself: *Is this action, person, or responsibility contributing to my higher purpose? Or is it draining my energy and focus?* If the answer is no, it may be time to reevaluate or let go.

6. Practice Patience and Trust the Process

Aligning your actions with your higher purpose is not always a quick or linear journey. Sometimes, the path forward will feel uncertain or challenging. Trust that the steps you are taking are leading you in the right direction, even if the results aren't immediately visible. Patience and perseverance are essential as you stay true to your purpose and continue taking intentional action.

Living a Purpose-Aligned Life

When you live in alignment with your higher purpose, your life becomes more meaningful and fulfilling. You wake up each day knowing that what you're doing matters and that you are making a positive impact, no matter how big or small. Your actions are no longer driven by fear or external expectations, but by a deep sense of inner knowing and authenticity.

To align your actions with your higher purpose is to live a life of intention. It's about knowing that every decision, every action, and every moment can contribute to the greater vision you've set for your life. By staying true to your purpose, you cultivate a life that feels authentic, meaningful, and deeply rewarding. When your actions reflect your higher purpose, you not only change your life—you change the world around you.

Creating Momentum and Staying Committed

One of the most crucial elements of achieving any dream, no matter how big or small, is the ability to **create momentum** and **stay committed** throughout the journey. Momentum is what propels you forward, even when obstacles arise or the initial excitement begins to fade. It's the energy and drive that build over time, pushing you through challenges and keeping you focused on your goals. Commitment, on the other hand, is the deep-rooted decision to stay the course, no matter how long or difficult the path may seem.

When you combine momentum with unwavering commitment, you create a powerful force that makes success not just possible but inevitable. The key to achieving anything is not about making huge leaps all at once; it's about **small, consistent actions** that accumulate over time, creating unstoppable forward motion.

The Importance of Momentum in Achieving Your Goals

Momentum is like a snowball rolling downhill—it starts small, but as it continues to move, it picks up speed, power, and force. Once you've created momentum, progress becomes easier, and you'll find yourself building on previous successes.

Here's why momentum is crucial:

1. **It Builds Confidence**: Every step forward, no matter how small, adds to your confidence. With each task you accomplish, you prove to yourself that you are capable and that progress is possible.

2. **It Overcomes Resistance**: In the beginning stages of any project or goal, resistance can feel overwhelming. Momentum helps you push past the initial inertia and get into the flow. Once you start taking action, the momentum helps you continue moving forward.

3. **It Makes Success Inevitable**: The longer you sustain momentum, the more difficult it becomes to stop. Success becomes a natural outcome of your persistent effort and forward motion. The longer you keep pushing forward, the greater your chances of achieving your desired result.

How to Create and Sustain Momentum

1. Start Small but Start Now

The most important thing is to begin. Often, we wait for the "perfect" moment or until we feel fully prepared, but the key is taking action **now**. Starting small is perfectly fine, and in fact, it's often the best way to begin. Small wins add up, creating positive reinforcement that encourages you to keep moving forward.

Ask yourself: What's the simplest step I can take today that will move me closer to my goal? It might be as simple as writing a paragraph, making one phone call, or reading a page of a book. **Action, no matter how small, creates momentum.**

2. Consistency Is Key

Consistency is what transforms small actions into big results. Committing to working on your goal every day, even for just a short amount of time, helps you build the momentum needed to achieve it. Consistency doesn't mean perfection—it means showing up, day after day, even when you don't feel like it, even when the results aren't immediate.

By focusing on daily actions rather than perfection, you remove the pressure and allow yourself to make steady progress. Set aside time each day to work on your goals, whether it's 10 minutes or an hour. Over time, these small efforts will add up and propel you forward.

3. Celebrate Every Win, Big or Small

Momentum thrives on positive reinforcement. Every time you achieve a goal or complete a task, take a moment to acknowledge your success. Celebrating wins, no matter how small, reinforces the progress you're making and boosts your motivation to keep going.

Celebrations could be as simple as acknowledging your progress, rewarding yourself with something meaningful, or sharing your success with someone who supports you. These small moments of recognition create a positive cycle, reinforcing your commitment and energizing your drive.

4. Stay Focused on the Bigger Picture

While momentum is built through consistent action, it's also important to stay connected to your **why**—the bigger picture of why you started in the first place. When you remember the deeper purpose behind your actions, it helps you stay motivated, even when you encounter setbacks or challenges.

Reflect regularly on your long-term vision and remind yourself of the values that are driving you. When you focus on the larger impact or the fulfilment you'll gain, it makes the daily grind more meaningful and worthwhile.

5. Push Through Setbacks and Challenges

Momentum doesn't mean that the journey will always be smooth. There will be obstacles, moments of doubt, and times when you feel like giving up. **Commitment is what keeps you going when momentum slows down**. It's the willingness to push through the difficult moments and continue taking action, even when the results aren't immediate.

It's in these moments of adversity that your commitment and determination are truly tested. Instead of letting setbacks discourage you, view them as opportunities to learn, grow, and become more resilient. Every challenge is a stepping stone to your ultimate success.

Staying Committed: The Power of Resilience

Commitment is the foundation that sustains momentum over the long haul. When you are deeply committed to your goals and vision, you are more likely to stick with them, even when things get tough. The ability to stay committed, especially during challenging times, is what sets successful people apart from those who give up along the way.

Here are some tips for staying committed:

1. **Reconnect with Your Purpose**: When you feel your commitment wavering, reconnect with the deeper reasons you set your goal in the first place. Ask yourself: *Why does this matter to me? What is the larger impact of my success?* This can reignite your motivation and recommit you to the path ahead.

2. **Set Milestones**: Break your big goal into smaller, manageable milestones. This helps you stay focused on short-term targets while also keeping your eye on the larger goal. Achieving these smaller milestones helps maintain momentum and keeps you committed.

3. **Stay Accountable**: Share your goals with someone who will hold you accountable. Whether it's a friend, mentor, or coach, having someone to check in with can reinforce your commitment and keep you on track. External accountability often provides the push you need to stay consistent and committed.

4. **Practice Patience**: Big goals take time, and progress isn't always linear. It's easy to get frustrated or discouraged if things don't happen as quickly as you'd like. However, commitment requires the ability to persevere through those moments and trust that the process will unfold as long as you continue to take consistent action.

Conclusion: Keep the Momentum Alive

Creating momentum and staying committed are essential elements of achieving any goal. Momentum makes it easier to keep moving forward, even in the face of challenges, while commitment ensures that you stay the course, no matter what. With a clear focus on your higher purpose and consistent, small actions taken every day, you'll not only create momentum but maintain it—transforming your dreams into reality.

Remember, success is rarely a sprint—it's a marathon. **Stay committed, trust the process, and celebrate every step forward. The momentum you create will carry you farther than you ever imagined.**

Practical Step: Develop a vision Board and Action Plan

Creating a vision board and an action plan is one of the most powerful ways to transform your limitless thinking into tangible, achievable results. These tools help you focus on your goals, clarify your desires, and take actionable steps toward the life you envision. They provide clarity, inspiration, and direction, acting as a constant reminder of where you're headed and the powerful potential you have to shape your future.

What is a Vision Board?

A vision board is a visual representation of your dreams, goals, and aspirations. It's a collage of images, quotes, and words that symbolize your desired future and the life you want to create. The purpose of a vision board is to focus your energy on your goals by immersing yourself in visuals that reflect what you want to manifest. It's a tool that taps into the power of visualization—a practice known to increase motivation, enhance focus, and prime your brain for success.

By creating a vision board, you're giving yourself a constant reminder of your limitless potential. It helps you stay motivated, especially when challenges arise, and it keeps you on track as you work toward your dreams.

Why You Need a Vision Board

1. **Clarifies Your Goals**: When you visualize your goals and dreams, it forces you to get specific about what you truly want. Whether it's career achievements, personal growth, relationships, or financial freedom, a vision board helps you define and visualize exactly what you're striving for.

2. **Increases Motivation**: Having a visual reminder of your goals keeps you inspired and focused. On days when you feel unmotivated or doubt your progress, a vision board reignites your passion and drives you to keep going.

3. **Boosts Positive Energy**: Surrounding yourself with images of what you desire boosts your positive energy and helps attract the opportunities, people, and resources you need to make your vision a reality.

4. **Reprograms Your Subconscious Mind**: Repeatedly viewing your vision board sends powerful messages to your subconscious mind. It helps align your beliefs with your goals, making you more open to the possibilities of success and abundance.

How to Create Your Vision Board

1. **Set Your Intentions**: Before starting your vision board, take a moment to reflect on what you truly desire in life. What do you want to achieve personally, professionally, and spiritually? Be clear and specific about your intentions.

2. **Gather Your Materials**: You can create a physical vision board using a corkboard or poster board, or you can go digital using a vision board app or software. For a physical board, gather magazines, printed images, scissors, glue, and markers. If you're working digitally, find inspiring images and design your board using a tool like Canva or Pinterest.

3. **Select Images and Words**: Choose images, words, and quotes that represent your goals. Look for visuals that evoke positive emotions and resonate with your deepest desires. Whether it's pictures of your dream house, the place you want to travel to, or words that inspire confidence, pick visuals that make you feel empowered and excited.

4. **Arrange and Create**: Once you have your images and words, start arranging them on your board. There's no right or wrong way to do this—let your creativity flow. When you look at your vision board, it should spark joy and inspiration. Feel free to make it colorful and vibrant, as this adds energy to your vision.

5. **Display Your Vision Board**: Once your vision board is complete, place it somewhere you'll see it every day—preferably somewhere visible in your home, office, or workspace. The more you interact with it, the more it will keep you motivated and focused on your goals.

Creating an Action Plan

A vision board alone is powerful, but it's the **action plan** that transforms your dreams into reality. The purpose of an action plan is to break down your goals into actionable steps, creating a roadmap that guides you toward your vision. This helps prevent overwhelm and ensures that you're consistently making progress.

Here's how to create an actionable plan that aligns with your vision:

1. **Define Your Big Goals**: Start by reviewing your vision board. What are the most important goals you want to focus on first? These might be related to career, relationships, health, or personal growth. Make sure they align with your larger vision and purpose.

2. **Break Down Your Goals into Smaller Steps**: A goal is much more achievable when you break it down into smaller, manageable tasks. For

example, if your vision includes starting your own business, your action plan could include steps like researching your industry, creating a business plan, setting up a website, and networking. Each of these steps brings you closer to your bigger goal.

3. **Set a Timeline**: Timeframes are essential to turning your vision into reality. Set realistic deadlines for each step of your action plan. This will help you stay focused and motivated, and provide you with a sense of urgency to keep moving forward.

4. **Prioritize**: Not all tasks will be equally important. Identify which steps have the most significant impact on achieving your goals and prioritize those. Focus on what will move you closer to your vision and tackle those first.

5. **Track Your Progress**: Keep track of your progress to stay accountable. Celebrate the small wins along the way to maintain your momentum. Regularly reviewing your progress helps you stay on track and make adjustments when necessary.

6. **Stay Flexible and Adapt**: Life rarely goes according to plan, and your journey toward your limitless life may involve unexpected detours. While it's important to stay focused, be flexible enough to adapt to changes or seize new opportunities that align with your vision. Your action plan should be a living document that evolves as you do.

Combining Your Vision Board with Your Action Plan

To achieve your limitless life, it's essential to **combine the power of your vision board** with a concrete, actionable plan. Your vision board serves as a constant source of inspiration, while your action plan ensures you take the necessary steps to make your dreams a reality.

Here's how to align both:

- **Use your vision board as a daily reminder** of where you want to go and why you're working toward your goals.

- **Review your action plan regularly** to ensure you're on track and making progress. Your vision board helps you see the bigger picture, and your action plan breaks it down into bite-sized pieces.

Conclusion: From Dreamer to Doer

Creating a vision board and action plan is a powerful way to manifest the limitless life you envision. By combining visual inspiration with strategic action, you build a strong foundation for turning your dreams into reality. The key to success lies in consistency, commitment, and aligning your daily actions with your grand vision.

With a clear vision and a detailed action plan, you'll move from being a dreamer to a doer, taking intentional steps toward the life you deserve. **Your limitless potential is waiting—start building it today.**

10

Living Limitlessly – Be the Person You Were Meant to Be

What a Limitless Life Looks Like

L iving a limitless life means stepping into your fullest potential and embracing the vast possibilities that lie before you. It's a life of abundance, freedom, and boundless opportunity—one where you are not constrained by fear, doubt, or limiting beliefs. A limitless life is not about having an absence of challenges, but rather, it's about approaching life with the confidence, resilience, and mindset that you have the power to create and navigate your own destiny.

A limitless life is marked by freedom—the freedom to live on your own terms, make bold decisions, and pursue your passions without hesitation. It's a life in which you have the courage to take risks, to fall and rise again, to move forward even when the road seems uncertain, and to believe in your ability to achieve extraordinary things. It's not just about achieving success in the conventional sense, but about creating a life that is authentic, fulfilling, and in alignment with who you are at your core.

Key Characteristics of a Limitless Life

1. Self-Confidence and Inner Peace

At the heart of a limitless life is a deep sense of **self-confidence**. This confidence isn't about being arrogant or without doubt; rather, it's the quiet assurance that you are enough, exactly as you are. You know that your worth is not defined by external validation, but by the truth of who you are and the unique gifts you bring to the world. This self-assurance fuels your decisions, your actions, and the way you navigate life.

189

When you live limitlessly, you also experience a sense of **inner peace**. You're not constantly chasing after the approval of others or seeking external markers of success. Instead, you feel grounded, centered, and in harmony with your own truth. You trust your intuition and make choices that align with your values, bringing a sense of peace that permeates every area of your life.

2. Freedom from Fear and Doubt

A limitless life is one in which you **fear less** and embrace growth more. Fear and self-doubt are no longer the driving forces behind your decisions; they don't hold you back from pursuing your dreams or making bold choices. You acknowledge fear as a natural human experience, but you don't let it control your actions or define your future.

Instead of seeing obstacles as threats, you view them as opportunities for **growth** and **learning**. You understand that setbacks aren't failures—they're stepping stones to success. You become resilient in the face of challenges and use them as fuel to grow stronger and wiser. Fear becomes something you can move through, not something that paralyzes you.

3. Purpose-Driven Living

Living limitlessly means living with **purpose**. You wake up every day with a clear sense of why you do what you do, knowing that your actions are aligned with your deepest values and desires. Your purpose guides your decisions and actions, fueling your motivation and providing a sense of fulfilment.

In a limitless life, you're not simply going through the motions. You're creating meaningful, intentional progress toward your goals, understanding that every step you take has a purpose. Whether it's your career, relationships, or personal growth, every aspect of your life is infused with intention and a deeper sense of meaning.

4. Abundance and Gratitude

A limitless life is one that is rooted in an **abundance mindset**. You no longer see the world through the lens of scarcity, where resources, opportunities, and success are limited. Instead, you believe that there is always more to be had—more opportunities, more resources, more success, more love. You know that there is enough for everyone, and that your success does not come at the expense of others.

This mindset leads to a deep sense of **gratitude**. You recognize the beauty in every moment, celebrate your achievements, and acknowledge the abundance that already exists in your life. By living in a state of gratitude, you open yourself up to receiving even more, and you create a positive, empowered environment around you. You become a magnet for opportunities, success, and positive experiences.

5. Empowered Relationships

Living limitlessly also means cultivating **empowered relationships**. These are relationships that nourish you, challenge you to grow, and support you on your journey. You surround yourself with people who uplift you, who encourage your growth, and who share your values. You have the confidence to set healthy boundaries, speak your truth, and engage in relationships that are reciprocal and fulfilling.

You also become the type of person who empowers others. When you live a limitless life, you naturally inspire and encourage those around you to step into their own greatness. You celebrate their successes as much as your own, knowing that their achievements do not diminish yours. In fact, the success of others becomes a reflection of your own abundance and growth.

6. Living in Alignment with Your Highest Self

A limitless life is a life that is fully **aligned** with your highest self. You no longer live based on societal expectations, other people's opinions, or external pressures. Instead, you follow your own path—one that reflects who you truly are and what you truly want out of life.

This alignment with your highest self brings a sense of fulfilment and clarity. You trust your intuition, and your actions reflect your inner wisdom and authenticity. You are no longer caught in the trap of comparison, feeling less than or not enough. You embrace your uniqueness, knowing that you are meant to shine in your own extraordinary way.

7. Joyful, Present Living

Finally, a limitless life is one filled with **joy** and a deep appreciation for the present moment. You don't wait for some distant future to start living fully; instead, you enjoy every step of the journey. You find joy in the small things—the warmth of the sun on your skin, the laughter of loved ones, the sense of accomplishment from taking small, consistent steps toward your goals.

Living limitlessly means being present, appreciating life as it is, and savoring every moment. It's a reminder that life isn't about waiting for everything to be perfect; it's about embracing the beauty and richness of the now.

Living Limitlessly: The Invitation

Living limitlessly is not reserved for a select few; it is available to anyone who is ready to step into their power, shed limiting beliefs, and embrace their potential. It's a journey of constant evolution—one that requires courage, resilience, and a deep trust in yourself and the process of life.

The limitless life is not a destination but a way of being. It is a life where you choose to embrace possibility over limitation, freedom over fear, and growth over stagnation. It is a life where you show up as the highest version of yourself, making a meaningful impact on the world and living with intention and purpose.

Are you ready to embrace your limitless life? The choice is yours, and the time is now.

The Power of Consistency in Building Lasting Change

When it comes to creating lasting change in your life, there's one principle that stands above all others: **consistency**. While most of us crave instant transformation or a quick fix, real and sustainable change takes time, effort, and unwavering commitment. The magic lies in showing up day after day, even when the excitement of the initial push begins to fade.

Consistency is the secret ingredient that turns dreams into reality. It's the steady, relentless action that compounds over time, ultimately leading to significant results. It's not about making huge leaps or achieving instant success; it's about doing the small things consistently—every single day—that build the foundation for real, lasting transformation.

Why Consistency is Key to Lasting Change

1. **It Builds Habits**

   At the core of lasting change is the formation of new habits. Whether you're working to shift your mindset, improve your health, build a successful career, or foster better relationships, the consistent actions you take are what help you build sustainable habits. Habits, once ingrained, become automatic, meaning the work you put in starts to feel effortless and less daunting. Over time, these habits begin to shape who you are, driving you to naturally align with your goals and values.

2. **It Creates Momentum**

   Momentum is a powerful force. When you consistently take action, no matter how small, you create forward motion in your life. You start seeing results, which fuels your motivation and gives you the drive to keep going. Even if the progress feels slow at first, consistency ensures that you don't lose sight of your goal. With each small step, you're building momentum that propels you toward your vision. **The more** you do, **the easier it becomes**—and soon, you'll realize that what once felt impossible is now a part of your reality.

3. **It Overcomes Obstacles**

Life will inevitably throw obstacles your way. Challenges, setbacks, and moments of doubt are part of the journey. But consistency helps you navigate these challenges without losing sight of your ultimate goal. When you stay consistent, even when things aren't going as planned, you develop resilience and the ability to persevere. **Consistency teaches you that success isn't about avoiding obstacles but learning to move through them**. The small, steady actions you take during tough times often lead to breakthroughs.

4. **It Reinforces Your Identity**

The more consistently you show up for yourself, the more your actions begin to shape your identity. When you repeatedly take action toward your goals, you start to see yourself as someone who is capable, driven, and committed. Your identity shifts from that of a person who *wants* to change to someone who *is* changing. This mental shift is crucial because **how you see yourself directly impacts your behavior**. As your identity changes, so do your actions, and so does the world around you.

5. **It Cultivates Patience and Persistence**

One of the most important lessons consistency teaches is patience. Transformations don't happen overnight, and the road to success is often winding and long. But consistency helps you develop the patience necessary to stay on track, even when the path feels slow. With persistence, you continue to show up, even on days when progress feels minimal. **Over time, this steady persistence leads to extraordinary results**, and you begin to understand that it's the journey—not just the destination—that's truly transformative.

How to Cultivate Consistency

1. **Start Small**

   Consistency doesn't require drastic changes all at once. In fact, starting small and setting manageable goals is the key to building a sustainable habit. Instead of committing to an unrealistic daily regimen, start with a few minutes each day. Over time, those minutes will grow, and what once seemed like a difficult habit to form will become second nature. Small wins accumulate, and with each win, you're building the muscle of consistency.

2. **Make It Non-Negotiable**

   Consistency is built when your actions become non-negotiable. This means you prioritize your new habit or goal, making it a non-debatable part of your daily life. Whether it's a morning routine, daily exercise, or time set aside for reflection, treat it as a commitment that you honor no matter what. **When something becomes non-negotiable, it moves from being optional to essential**, and that mindset shift is crucial for consistency.

3. **Track Your Progress**

   Sometimes, the results of consistency can take time to manifest. That's why tracking your progress is important. Whether it's journaling, using a habit tracker, or simply noting your achievements, tracking helps you see how far you've come and reinforces the positive behaviors you're building. **Celebrate the small wins** along the way—this will keep you motivated and make it easier to stay consistent.

4. **Create Accountability**

   Accountability can play a huge role in maintaining consistency. Share your goals with someone you trust, whether it's a friend, family member, or mentor. Knowing that someone is checking in on your progress can provide the extra push you need to stay on track. Alternatively, you can join a group or community with similar goals for mutual support and encouragement.

5. **Embrace Imperfection**

It's easy to become discouraged when you miss a day or fall off track, but perfection is not the goal—progress is. Don't let a mistake or setback derail your efforts. Embrace the idea that life happens, and sometimes you'll miss a step. What matters is getting back on track as quickly as possible. **Consistency is about showing up over and over again, even if you stumble along the way**. Keep going, and you'll build the lasting change you desire.

The Compound Effect of Consistency

The most powerful thing about consistency is the compound effect. Just like the small actions you take each day add up to create lasting habits, the accumulation of those habits leads to significant transformation. It's like the snowball effect—what starts small grows bigger and bigger over time.

A daily habit of reading for just 10 minutes can lead to reading dozens of books over the course of a year. A few minutes of gratitude practice each morning can shift your entire mindset toward positivity and abundance. Consistently showing up for your goals—whether it's exercising, writing, or working on a project—compounds to create a life that reflects your deepest desires.

Conclusion: The Power of Consistency

In the end, the power of consistency lies in its ability to turn small, everyday actions into monumental, lasting change. **Consistency is the bridge between where you are now and the life you've always wanted.** It's the key to building habits, overcoming obstacles, and making progress—even when the road gets tough. Through consistency, you develop resilience, patience, and the unwavering belief that your dreams are within reach.

When you embrace consistency, you understand that transformation is not about grand gestures or sudden breakthroughs—it's about the quiet, steady commitment to showing up each day, doing the work, and trusting that the change you desire is already unfolding, one small step at a time.

Embracing Growth and Continuous Self-Improvement

At the heart of a limitless life lies a powerful and transformative mindset: the willingness to embrace growth and commit to continuous self-improvement. True transformation isn't about reaching a single destination, but about constantly evolving into the best version of yourself. Growth becomes a lifelong pursuit, a journey of learning, adapting, and expanding—both mentally and emotionally. The moment you embrace growth, you open the door to endless possibilities, uncovering the potential for greatness that resides within you.

Growth is not just about achieving goals; it's about becoming the person capable of achieving those goals. Every experience, every challenge, and every success contributes to your growth, shaping your mindset, enhancing your skills, and refining your character. When you choose to see growth as an ongoing process, you start to view obstacles not as setbacks but as opportunities to learn, improve, and elevate your life.

The Power of a Growth Mindset

A growth mindset is the foundation of personal development. Coined by psychologist Carol Dweck, the concept of a growth mindset revolves around the belief that your abilities, intelligence, and talents can be developed through hard work, dedication, and learning. People with a growth mindset view challenges as opportunities to grow rather than threats to their success. They understand that failures are not permanent, but stepping stones on the path to mastery.

This mindset shifts how you approach all aspects of life. It encourages you to **take risks**, **embrace challenges**, and **persevere** when things get tough. When you adopt a growth mindset, you move away from a fixed perspective that limits you and embrace the freedom of knowing that **you can always improve**.

Key Characteristics of a Growth Mindset:

- **Learning from mistakes**: Instead of viewing failure as a reflection of your inadequacy, you see it as a lesson—a valuable opportunity to grow.

- **Resilience**: Challenges don't define you; they refine you. With a growth mindset, you bounce back stronger, more determined, and better equipped to handle future obstacles.

- **Curiosity and openness**: You become a lifelong learner, constantly seeking knowledge, developing new skills, and expanding your understanding of the world and yourself.

Why Continuous Self-Improvement is Crucial

Continuous self-improvement is essential because growth doesn't happen by accident—it happens by **intention and effort**. When you commit to constantly bettering yourself, you don't just wait for change to come to you. You actively seek out the opportunities, tools, and mindsets that will allow you to grow.

1. **Increases Self-Awareness**

   The journey of self-improvement begins with **self-awareness**—the ability to honestly assess where you are in life and where you want to go. By continuously improving yourself, you become more in tune with your strengths, weaknesses, values, and desires. This heightened self-awareness helps you make better decisions, align your actions with your purpose, and create a life that's truly in harmony with who you are. It encourages introspection and a deeper understanding of the thoughts, emotions, and behaviors that shape your life.

2. **Fosters Confidence and Self-Worth**

   As you improve yourself, you prove to yourself that you are capable of growth and change. Every step forward, no matter how small, builds your **self-confidence**. You begin to trust in your ability to tackle challenges and rise above limitations. This belief in your ability to grow creates a positive feedback loop, fueling your desire to keep learning, evolving, and striving for greatness.

3. **Enhances Your Relationships**

   When you focus on personal growth, you become more empathetic, patient, and compassionate. You learn to communicate more effectively, resolve conflicts with grace, and build deeper, more meaningful connections. Personal growth fosters emotional intelligence, which enhances both professional and personal relationships, allowing you to create a positive environment that attracts success and fulfilment.

4. Increases Resilience to Challenges

Life is unpredictable, and challenges are inevitable. But when you embrace the mindset of continuous growth, you become more resilient in the face of adversity. **Self-improvement helps you develop the skills and emotional strength** to deal with stress, setbacks, and obstacles. Rather than succumbing to frustration or discouragement, you find ways to adjust, learn, and move forward. Your ability to bounce back stronger after facing challenges becomes a powerful testament to your growth.

5. Keeps You Engaged and Motivated

Self-improvement fuels motivation because it creates a sense of progress. As you learn new things, acquire new skills, or make strides toward your goals, you feel a sense of accomplishment that propels you forward. You recognize that the process of growing and improving is as important as the destination itself, which keeps you engaged in the journey and motivated to keep going. It's this consistent momentum that leads to a life of fulfilment and success.

How to Cultivate Continuous Self-Improvement

1. Set Clear, Actionable Goals

Self-improvement doesn't happen without a plan. By setting clear, specific, and actionable goals, you create a roadmap for your personal growth journey. Break down large goals into smaller, manageable steps, and regularly assess your progress. Goals provide direction and purpose, making the process of improvement intentional and measurable.

2. **Commit to Lifelong Learning**

   Commit yourself to being a lifelong learner. Whether through reading, taking courses, attending workshops, or engaging in new experiences, always seek opportunities to expand your knowledge and skillset. The more you learn, the more you grow, and the more equipped you are to handle the challenges life throws your way.

3. **Embrace Feedback**

   Growth happens through feedback. Whether from others or from self-reflection, constructive criticism helps you identify areas for improvement. Rather than being defensive or dismissing feedback, **embrace it as a valuable tool** for growth. Use it as a guide to refine your skills, change your approach, and become better at what you do.

4. **Take Consistent Action**

   Improvement comes from action. It's not enough to simply think about change or read about it in books. You must take consistent, deliberate steps to improve yourself each day. It's the small, consistent actions that compound over time and lead to substantial change. Whether it's practicing a new skill, adopting a healthy habit, or working toward a goal, consistency is key to continual growth.

5. **Celebrate Progress, Not Perfection**

   Growth isn't about perfection—it's about progress. Celebrate every step forward, no matter how small. This reinforces the habit of improvement and encourages you to continue striving for greater heights. Remember, perfection is not the goal; **becoming the best version of yourself** is what truly matters.

Conclusion: The Lifelong Journey of Growth

Embracing growth and continuous self-improvement is an ongoing process—one that requires commitment, perseverance, and a willingness to embrace the discomfort of change. **Growth is not a destination, but a journey** that shapes who you are, who you become, and the life you create. The more you invest in your personal development, the more you open yourself up to new possibilities, deeper fulfilment, and greater success.

When you choose to embrace growth, you become empowered to transform your life, one step at a time. And as you evolve, you not only improve your own life, but you also inspire others to do the same. The journey of continuous self-improvement is not only about reaching your potential; it's about **living out your limitless potential** each and every day.

How to Maintain Your Limitless Thinking for a Lifetime

Creating a limitless mindset is an empowering transformation, but the real challenge lies in maintaining it over the long term. The initial enthusiasm of change can be easy to sustain, but how do you keep that spark alive and continue to thrive with limitless thinking, even when life gets complicated, or obstacles arise? The key is to develop habits and practices that reinforce your growth mindset and keep you aligned with your highest potential. By nurturing your mindset and remaining committed to your personal evolution, you can continue to live a life filled with boundless possibilities.

Here's how to maintain your limitless thinking for a lifetime:

1. Keep Reaffirming Your Vision and Purpose

Your vision and purpose are your guiding lights—they give your life direction and meaning. But as time passes, it's easy to get caught up in the day-to-day grind and lose sight of your bigger goals. To maintain a limitless mindset, you must regularly reconnect with your "why." This deepens your commitment to the journey and reminds you of the power and potential you hold within.

How to maintain your vision:

- **Create a vision board**: Visual representation of your goals and dreams can serve as a daily reminder of your aspirations.

- **Write a purpose statement**: Reaffirm your purpose by writing a brief statement about why you do what you do. Reflect on this often.

- **Set long-term and short-term goals**: Break your big vision into smaller milestones. Celebrate each step forward, knowing that every achievement is part of a larger purpose.

2. Cultivate a Practice of Self-Reflection

Self-reflection is a powerful tool for maintaining a limitless mindset because it keeps you aware of your thoughts, actions, and progress. By reflecting regularly on your experiences and growth, you reinforce your commitment to limitless thinking and make adjustments as needed.

How to engage in self-reflection:

- **Daily journaling**: Take a few minutes each day to reflect on your thoughts, actions, and feelings. What went well today? What can you improve tomorrow? Journaling helps you stay in touch with your inner thoughts and keeps you focused on positive growth.

- **Monthly check-ins**: Every month, evaluate where you are in relation to your goals. Are you moving forward or getting distracted? What needs to shift in your mindset or actions to stay on course?

- **Mindfulness practices**: Meditation, breathing exercises, or simply taking a walk can help you clear your mind and gain clarity on your life's direction.

3. Surround Yourself with Supportive Influences

The people you interact with have a profound impact on your mindset. To maintain a limitless way of thinking, it's essential to surround yourself with positive, like-minded individuals who encourage your growth, challenge your limiting beliefs, and celebrate your successes.

How to surround yourself with positive influences:

- **Join a mastermind group or community**: Being part of a group that shares similar goals and values can help you stay motivated and inspired. The collective energy of growth-minded individuals can amplify your own progress.

- **Limit negative influences**: Distance yourself from individuals or environments that reinforce limiting beliefs or hold you back from your potential. This might mean setting boundaries with people who are stuck in a fixed mindset or who constantly bring negativity into your life.

- **Seek mentors and role models**: Find people who inspire you and learn from their experiences. A mentor can offer valuable guidance and help you stay focused on your limitless journey.

4. Embrace Lifelong Learning

A limitless mindset thrives in an environment of constant learning and curiosity. The world is always evolving, and so should you. Continuously challenging your mind and expanding your knowledge helps you break free from stagnation and ensures that your thinking stays expansive and open.

How to keep learning:

- **Read regularly**: Books, articles, and podcasts offer endless opportunities for learning. Choose resources that challenge your perspectives, expand your knowledge, and spark new ideas.

- **Take courses and workshops**: Whether it's related to your career or personal interests, investing in learning keeps you mentally sharp and continually evolving.

- **Stay curious**: Always ask questions and seek answers. A mindset of curiosity will keep your thinking open and prevent you from falling into rigid patterns.

5. Develop Resilience to Setbacks

No journey toward limitless thinking is without its challenges. Life will inevitably throw obstacles your way. However, your ability to face setbacks with resilience is what determines whether your limitless mindset will endure. When you view challenges as opportunities to learn and grow, you shift your focus from fear to empowerment.

How to stay resilient:

- **Reframe setbacks as learning opportunities**: When faced with failure, ask yourself: "What can I learn from this?" Shift your perspective from disappointment to curiosity.

- **Practice gratitude**: Even in the face of difficulties, find something to be grateful for. Gratitude helps shift your mindset from scarcity to abundance, allowing you to find opportunities in every situation.

- **Keep a growth journal**: Write down challenges you've faced and how you overcame them. Reflecting on past successes in the face of adversity helps build confidence in your ability to handle future setbacks.

6. Take Consistent Action Toward Your Goals

To maintain a limitless mindset, you must keep moving forward with intention. Limitless thinking requires action. Every day, take small steps toward your big vision, and over time, those steps will add up to incredible progress. It's easy to get distracted or discouraged, but the key is to keep moving, even if it's just a little bit each day.

How to maintain consistent action:

- **Create daily habits**: Incorporate small, positive actions into your routine that support your bigger goals. Whether it's exercising, journaling, or learning something new, small daily actions keep you on track.

- **Track your progress**: Keep a record of your wins, however small they may seem. This helps you stay motivated and reinforces the belief that your efforts are paying off.

- **Stay accountable**: Whether through a mentor, friend, or personal accountability partner, having someone to check in with ensures you remain committed to your path.

7. Celebrate Your Wins and Reflect on Your Growth

Finally, it's important to regularly pause and celebrate your wins—no matter how big or small. When you acknowledge your achievements, you reinforce the power of limitless thinking and set the stage for even greater accomplishments.

How to celebrate and reflect:

- **Create a victory ritual**: Take time to reflect on your progress and celebrate your milestones. This reinforces the idea that growth is continuous and worth acknowledging.

- **Document your journey**: Reflect on your transformation and how far you've come. Documenting your journey helps you see the progress you've made, which inspires you to keep going.

Conclusion: The Lifelong Commitment to Limitless Thinking

Maintaining a limitless mindset for a lifetime is not about perfection or reaching an endpoint—it's about the continual commitment to growth, learning, and taking action toward your dreams. When you remain intentional, resilient, and connected to your purpose, your limitless thinking will not only endure but flourish.

By cultivating a practice of reflection, surrounding yourself with supportive influences, and embracing lifelong learning, you create an environment where your limitless potential can thrive. Remember, this is your journey, and **every small step forward is a victory**. Keep believing in yourself, stay true to your vision, and embrace the limitless possibilities that await you.

Practical Step: Creating Your Limitless Future Map

One of the most powerful tools you can use to turn your limitless thinking into reality is creating a *Limitless Future Map*. This map acts as both a **roadmap** and a **vision** for your life, a visual representation of your goals, aspirations, and the person you are becoming. It serves as a guiding framework to help you align your daily actions with your long-term dreams, ensuring that you remain focused and inspired on your path to limitless success.

Creating a Limitless Future Map is more than just a to-do list; it's a dynamic, actionable, and evolving plan that grows with you. Here's how to craft your own Limitless Future Map, step-by-step:

1. Define Your Vision for the Future

Start by taking time to reflect on the bigger picture of your life. What does your ideal future look like? What are your dreams and aspirations, both personally and professionally? Imagine yourself five or even ten years from now—what kind of person are you? What achievements have you unlocked? What impact are you making on the world?

Action Steps:

- **Visualize your future**: Close your eyes and imagine your perfect life. What do you see? What does it feel like? Where are you? Who are you surrounded by? What are you doing? Use this exercise to tap into your deepest desires and create a clear vision.

- **Write it down**: Once you've visualized your future, write it down in as much detail as possible. Be specific about what you want in various areas of your life—career, relationships, health, finances, personal growth, and beyond.

- **Make it bold and inspiring**: Your vision should excite you. Let it be a reflection of your highest potential and the life you want to create. This is your personal declaration of what's possible for you.

2. Break Down Your Vision into Specific Goals

Now that you have a clear vision of your limitless future, it's time to break it down into actionable goals. Think of these as the milestones that will guide you toward your ultimate vision. Break your goals into short-term, mid-term, and long-term objectives. This ensures that you can celebrate smaller successes along the way while staying focused on the bigger picture.

Action Steps:

- **Set SMART goals**: For each area of your vision, set specific, measurable, attainable, relevant, and time-bound goals. For example, if your vision includes being a successful entrepreneur, your SMART goal could be to launch a business within the next year.

- **Prioritize**: Identify the most important goals that will have the greatest impact on your life. These should be your focus, while other smaller goals can support your bigger objectives.

- **Write your goals**: Once you've identified your goals, write them down, and be as specific as possible. For example, "I will start my own business" can be expanded into "I will research and finalize a business plan within the next 6 months."

3. Map Out the Milestones

Once you've set your goals, the next step is to map out the milestones you'll need to hit to achieve each goal. These are the smaller, actionable steps that will help you stay on track and measure your progress.

Action Steps:

- **Break down your goals**: For each goal, list the smaller tasks or actions required to make it happen. For instance, if one of your goals is to improve your health, the milestones could include "sign up for a gym membership," "hire a personal trainer," or "set a weekly meal prep routine."

- **Set deadlines**: Assign realistic deadlines for each milestone. Deadlines create a sense of urgency and prevent procrastination, helping you stay motivated and focused.

- **Keep it flexible**: Life is unpredictable, so while having a plan is crucial, remember that milestones can be adjusted as you go. Allow space for new opportunities, challenges, or learning experiences.

4. Visualize Your Map

Your Limitless Future Map should be something that you can physically see every day, keeping your goals and aspirations front and center. This can be done through a vision board, a digital roadmap, or a detailed written plan—whatever form resonates with you most.

Action Steps:

- **Create a vision board**: A vision board is a powerful visual representation of your dreams and goals. Gather images, words, and quotes that represent your future and arrange them on a board or poster. This daily visual reminder can keep you inspired and focused.

- **Use a digital map**: If you prefer a digital approach, create a document or slide presentation that outlines your goals, milestones, and visual cues. This can easily be accessed on your phone or computer to keep you connected to your vision at all times.

- **Place it where you can see it**: Whether it's your vision board on the wall, a planner on your desk, or a digital reminder on your phone, ensure that your Limitless Future Map is something you engage with regularly to stay focused on your journey.

5. Take Consistent Action

The most important part of your Limitless Future Map is the action you take to make it a reality. While visualization and planning are essential, it's the daily habits and consistent action that will ultimately bring your dreams to life.

Action Steps:

- **Commit to daily actions**: Break your larger tasks into bite-sized actions that you can take every day. This could be as simple as reading for 20 minutes, working on your business plan for an hour, or journaling your thoughts on growth.

- **Track your progress**: Keep a journal or progress tracker to record your achievements and how you're advancing toward your goals. This allows you to celebrate victories and identify areas where you may need to adjust your plan.

- **Adjust as necessary**: Sometimes life throws curveballs, and your plans may need to evolve. Don't be afraid to adjust your map if something isn't working. Flexibility is key in maintaining a limitless mindset.

6. Reflect and Review Regularly

Your Limitless Future Map is a living, breathing document. To keep yourself on track, make it a habit to regularly review and reflect on your goals and progress. This reflection process allows you to celebrate wins, learn from setbacks, and make necessary adjustments to keep moving forward.

Action Steps:

- **Weekly reviews**: Every week, set aside time to review your progress, assess how far you've come, and reflect on what's working and what's not. This keeps you aligned with your path and ensures that you're moving forward consistently.

- **Adjust goals as needed**: Over time, your goals may evolve or shift as you grow. If your vision changes, update your map accordingly to ensure that it remains relevant to where you are and where you want to go.

Conclusion: Your Limitless Future Starts Now

Creating a Limitless Future Map is not just about setting goals; it's about aligning your daily actions with the life you want to create. By visualizing your future, breaking down your goals into actionable steps, and regularly reviewing your progress, you maintain a constant focus on growth and success.

Remember, this map isn't a static blueprint—it's a living, evolving plan that grows with you. The more you engage with it, the more clarity you'll have on how to make your limitless future a reality. Your journey toward living a limitless life starts with intention, commitment, and belief in your potential. Let your Limitless Future Map be the roadmap that guides you every step of the way.

Conclusion: Your Journey Has Just Begun

Reflecting on Your Transformation

As we reach the final pages of this journey, it's important to pause and reflect on the profound transformation you've undergone. Change doesn't happen overnight, but every small step you've taken, every mindset shift, and every courageous action has brought you closer to the limitless version of yourself you're becoming.

Look back at where you started—perhaps you felt uncertain, held back by doubts, or trapped by limiting beliefs. Now, as you stand at the threshold of a new chapter, take a moment to recognize how far you've come. You've already begun to rewire your brain, embrace failure as a stepping stone, and tap into the infinite potential that resides within you. This is not the end of your journey; it's a pivotal moment of reflection and celebration, a moment to honor the progress you've made.

Key Reflections on Your Journey:

1. **Recognizing Your Growth**

   Take a moment to look at your mindset and personal growth. When you started, you may have had doubts about your abilities. Now, you've cultivated a mindset of possibility, courage, and abundance. You've learned how to shift your thinking, break free from the limitations that once held you back, and embrace a new, empowered perspective. Your transformation is not just in your actions, but in the way you think, see the world, and interact with it.

2. **Celebrating Your Courage to Change**

Transformation requires bravery. It's not always easy to step out of your comfort zone, to confront your fears, and to take actions that challenge the status quo of your life. But you've done it. You've chosen to believe in your potential, to act on your dreams, and to persevere when things felt difficult. That courage is what has set you apart and propelled you forward.

3. **Recognizing the Power of Choice**

Throughout this journey, you've learned that the power to shape your reality lies within the choices you make. Whether you were faced with challenges or opportunities, the ability to choose how you respond has been your greatest strength. Each choice you've made, no matter how small, has contributed to the person you are becoming and the life you are creating.

4. **Embracing a Life of Possibility**

The most beautiful aspect of your transformation is the openness to the limitless possibilities ahead of you. Once confined by fear, scarcity, or self-doubt, you now stand on the other side, filled with the belief that anything is possible. You've learned that life is not a series of rigid outcomes, but a canvas upon which you paint your own masterpiece. You are free to create, explore, and evolve in ways you may never have thought possible before.

5. **The Momentum You've Created**

The habits, practices, and mindset shifts you've cultivated throughout this process have set the foundation for lifelong growth. The momentum you've gained will continue to carry you forward. As you continue to apply what you've learned, you will find that the path you've created will only become clearer and more rewarding with each passing day.

The Journey Is Just Beginning

This is not a conclusion—it's the beginning of a new chapter in your life. The tools, insights, and practices you've discovered here are only the start of your limitless journey. As you continue to evolve, remember that growth is not a destination, but a way of life. Keep revisiting your vision, realigning your actions with your purpose, and staying committed to the endless possibilities that lie ahead.

You have the power to shape your future with the thoughts you think, the choices you make, and the actions you take. Trust in the process, stay aligned with your vision, and remember that transformation is ongoing. With every new challenge, you have the opportunity to evolve into a stronger, more empowered version of yourself.

So, as you close this chapter, remember this: **Your journey has just begun.** Keep going. Keep dreaming. Keep believing. The world is waiting for you to live your limitless life.

The Ongoing Process of Becoming Limitless

Becoming limitless is not a one-time event—it's a continual, dynamic process. It's a journey of growth, transformation, and self-discovery that unfolds over time. As you step into your limitless potential, remember that you are constantly evolving. There will be moments of breakthroughs, but also periods of challenge. The beauty of this journey is that every experience, every lesson, and every setback is an opportunity to refine and deepen your capacity to live without limits.

The path to a limitless life is never linear. It's filled with twists and turns, with peaks of achievement and valleys of reflection. But what matters most is your commitment to the ongoing process of becoming the person you were always meant to be.

1. Embrace the Continuous Growth Mindset

To be limitless is to understand that growth doesn't have a finish line. It's about adopting a mindset that is always seeking improvement and expansion. While it's natural to desire a sense of completion or finality, the real joy lies in the journey of becoming. Embrace each day as an opportunity to evolve, learn, and stretch beyond your current limits.

Action Steps to Cultivate Growth:

- **Commit to lifelong learning**: Stay curious and continue exploring new ideas, concepts, and skills. Whether through books, courses, or conversations, commit to expanding your mind and perspective.

- **Welcome challenges**: Instead of shying away from difficulties, see them as opportunities to grow stronger. Each challenge is a chance to learn something new about yourself and the world around you.

- **Reflect regularly**: Take time to check in with yourself and your progress. Celebrate your achievements, but also identify areas for growth. This reflection helps you stay aligned with your evolving vision.

2. Redefine Failure as Feedback

In the pursuit of a limitless life, failure will inevitably come your way. But instead of seeing failure as an obstacle, view it as valuable feedback. Every "failure" offers insight into what works, what doesn't, and what needs to be adjusted. When you redefine failure as part of your process of growth, you open yourself up to learning rather than retreating.

Action Steps to Reframe Failure:

- **Analyze setbacks**: When faced with a challenge or setback, ask yourself: What can I learn from this? How can I adjust my approach moving forward?

- **Celebrate the lessons**: Each setback contains valuable lessons that can accelerate your growth. Rather than being discouraged, embrace failure as part of your journey.

- **Use failure to pivot**: If something doesn't work, pivot your approach. Look for ways to innovate and approach the situation with a fresh perspective.

3. Keep Expanding Your Vision

As you grow, your vision will expand. What once felt like a distant dream will become a reality, and new desires will take their place. The process of becoming limitless is rooted in the continual expansion of what you believe is possible. Every time you reach one milestone, it will unlock even greater potential within you. The key is to keep stretching your imagination and embracing new possibilities.

Action Steps to Expand Your Vision:

- **Revisit your goals**: Regularly assess your goals to ensure they align with your growth and evolving vision. Set new, bigger goals that push your boundaries.

- **Challenge your limits**: Push yourself to think bigger, act bolder, and reach higher than you thought possible. The more you stretch your vision, the more you'll expand your potential.

- **Surround yourself with inspiring influences**: Connect with people who have accomplished what you dream of, who challenge you to think beyond your current limits.

4. Develop Resilience and Patience

While the idea of limitless thinking can feel exhilarating, the reality is that transformation requires patience and resilience. It's easy to get discouraged when progress feels slow or setbacks seem overwhelming. But true greatness is built over time, and each step forward, no matter how small, is part of the process.

Action Steps to Build Resilience:

- **Develop emotional intelligence**: Work on managing your emotions, especially when facing adversity. Emotional resilience is key to staying on course despite challenges.

- **Practice patience**: Recognize that change takes time. Stay committed to your vision, knowing that each effort you make is getting you closer to your limitless future.

- **Stay focused on the long term**: Instead of getting caught up in day-to-day frustrations, remind yourself of the bigger picture. Trust that consistent, small actions will eventually lead to monumental progress.

5. Cultivate Daily Empowering Practices

Consistency is the secret ingredient that makes a limitless mindset sustainable. The small, daily habits you create will reinforce your vision and mindset, turning them into automatic behaviors that support your limitless way of being. These daily practices should nourish your body, mind, and spirit, keeping you aligned with your higher self and purpose.

Action Steps to Cultivate Consistency:

- **Daily affirmations**: Reinforce your limitless beliefs by affirming them every day. Affirm your worth, your potential, and your ability to overcome any obstacle.

- **Visualization**: Spend a few minutes each day visualizing your ideal life and the steps you need to take to get there. See yourself thriving, achieving, and becoming the person you are meant to be.

- **Gratitude practice**: Start each day by acknowledging the things you are grateful for. Gratitude helps you stay in an abundance mindset, attracting more of what you want into your life.

6. Trust in the Process

Finally, to continue your journey of becoming limitless, you must trust the process. The path is not always clear, and you may not always know the exact next step. But as long as you stay aligned with your vision, remain committed to your growth, and take consistent action, the right opportunities will present themselves. Trust that everything is unfolding as it should, and that your efforts are building toward something greater.

Action Steps to Strengthen Your Trust:

- **Let go of perfectionism**: Understand that progress is messy, and growth is not always linear. Trust that each step, even the missteps, is part of your greater evolution.

- **Stay present**: Focus on the journey rather than obsessing over the destination. Enjoy the process of becoming the person you were meant to be.

- **Believe in the power of time**: Know that all the work you're putting in today will pay off in the future. Trust that your limitless future is already being created with every action you take.

Conclusion: The Endless Journey of Limitless Living

The process of becoming limitless is not a goal to be reached—it's a lifelong journey. It is an ongoing evolution of your mindset, habits, and actions. By embracing continuous growth, redefining failure, expanding your vision, cultivating resilience, and staying consistent, you can live a life that is not confined by limitations. You have the power to shape your reality and unlock your potential at every turn.

Remember, the journey never truly ends. There will always be new heights to reach, new versions of yourself to become, and new ways to grow. **So keep going. Keep dreaming. Keep expanding.** The process of becoming limitless is ongoing, and the best is yet to come.

Embracing Life's Possibilities with Courage and Joy

Life is filled with infinite possibilities, yet many of us limit ourselves due to fear, self-doubt, or uncertainty about the future. But the truth is, we are capable of so much more than we often give ourselves credit for. To truly live a limitless life, it's essential to embrace the boundless opportunities around us with courage and joy.

Living a life filled with possibility doesn't mean that everything will be perfect or easy. It means being open to the unknown, stepping into new experiences, and trusting that every challenge holds the potential for growth. It's about daring to live fully, embracing the journey, and finding joy in the process, even when the outcome is unclear. By shifting your perspective to see life's challenges as opportunities, you unlock the power to turn every moment into a stepping stone toward your highest self.

Courage: The Key to Unlocking Possibility

Courage is not the absence of fear; it is the willingness to act in spite of it. Every step you take toward a new possibility requires courage—the courage to step out of your comfort zone, to try something new, and to face the unknown with confidence. It's easy to stay where it's safe and familiar, but true growth happens when you dare to venture beyond the boundaries you've set for yourself.

When you embrace life's possibilities with courage, you open yourself up to new adventures, experiences, and relationships that you might have once overlooked. Whether it's pursuing a new career, starting a passion project, or traveling to a new place, courage empowers you to seize opportunities that may have once seemed out of reach. With courage, you become the person who says yes to life, even when it feels uncertain or daunting.

Action Steps to Cultivate Courage:

- **Face your fears head-on**: Start small by doing one thing every day that challenges your comfort zone. It could be having a difficult conversation, learning a new skill, or making a bold decision.

- **Take imperfect action**: Don't wait for everything to be perfect. Courage means stepping forward even when you don't have all the answers.

- **Surround yourself with support**: Find people who uplift you, inspire you, and encourage your growth. A supportive environment will give you the strength to take brave actions.

Joy: The Fuel for Living Limitlessly

Joy is not just a fleeting emotion; it is a powerful energy that fuels us to take bold actions and keep going even when challenges arise. When you approach life with joy, you begin to see every moment as an opportunity for growth and adventure. It's about embracing the present with a sense of wonder and gratitude, finding delight in both the big milestones and the small moments.

Joy also brings a sense of freedom. It allows you to let go of the perfectionism and pressures that often hold us back, enabling you to approach life with a lighter heart and a more open mind. When you find joy in the process, you stop focusing solely on the end goal and begin to appreciate the journey itself. This shift in mindset is key to living a limitless life because it turns every experience—whether easy or challenging—into something enriching.

Action Steps to Cultivate Joy:

- **Practice gratitude daily**: Take a few moments each day to reflect on what you are grateful for. A gratitude practice shifts your focus to the positive, making it easier to find joy in every situation.

- **Celebrate small wins**: Don't wait for big achievements to feel joy. Celebrate the little victories—completing a task, stepping out of your comfort zone, or simply enjoying a quiet moment. These small moments of joy build up to create a fulfilling life.

- **Find joy in the present moment**: Practice mindfulness to stay present in the here and now. Life is happening right now, and joy is found when you are fully immersed in the moment, rather than looking to the past or future.

Living a Life of Limitless Possibility

When you combine courage with joy, you unlock the true potential of what's possible for your life. You stop holding yourself back, and instead, you lean into the opportunities that come your way. Life becomes a series of exciting possibilities rather than a series of challenges to endure. Every experience, every person you meet, and every lesson you learn contributes to the adventure of living limitlessly.

You begin to see that failure is just a lesson in disguise, setbacks are opportunities to rise, and each day is a fresh canvas to create something extraordinary. With courage, you no longer fear the unknown, and with joy, you approach every new chapter with a sense of wonder and excitement. You embrace each possibility with an open heart, trusting that no matter where the path leads, it will take you to places you never imagined possible.

Conclusion: Step into the Limitless Life

To embrace life's possibilities with courage and joy is to live without hesitation, to take bold actions, and to find beauty in every moment. It's about trusting yourself, the process, and the limitless potential that lies within you. So, take a deep breath, step forward with courage, and embrace the joy that comes with the unknown. Your limitless life is waiting for you to live it fully. The possibilities are endless, and the best part is, you get to choose how you will experience them.

How to Keep Nurturing Your Limitless Mindset

A limitless mindset is not something that is achieved and then left to stand on its own. It is a living, breathing aspect of who you are, constantly evolving and growing as you continue on your journey. To maintain and nurture this mindset, you must actively cultivate it, reinforcing the belief that you are capable of extraordinary things—no matter the obstacles you face. Just like a plant that requires sunlight, water, and care to thrive, your mindset needs consistent attention and nurturing to stay strong and expansive.

1. Stay Committed to Growth

A limitless mindset thrives on continuous growth. It's the understanding that no matter where you are in life, there is always room to expand, learn, and improve. This commitment to growth means embracing new challenges, seeking out knowledge, and refusing to settle into a fixed mindset. A growth-oriented approach allows you to remain open to the lessons life presents and understand that even setbacks are part of the bigger picture.

Action Steps:

- **Set new goals regularly**: Always aim for new milestones in your personal, professional, and spiritual growth. Push yourself beyond what you've already accomplished.

- **Commit to lifelong learning**: Take courses, read books, and surround yourself with people who challenge and inspire you. Every new piece of knowledge you gain is a brick in the foundation of your limitless mindset.

2. Practice Gratitude Every Day

Gratitude is one of the most powerful tools for maintaining a limitless mindset. When you focus on the things you're thankful for, it shifts your energy and perspective, helping you to see the abundance that already exists in your life. By consistently practicing gratitude, you train your mind to recognize the positive and abundant aspects of your reality rather than focusing on what you lack.

Action Steps:

- **Write a gratitude journal**: Spend a few minutes every day listing things you are grateful for. This could be big accomplishments or small daily joys.

- **Express your gratitude**: Tell others how much you appreciate them. Whether it's a simple thank-you note or a heartfelt message, expressing gratitude strengthens your mindset and keeps it grounded in positivity.

3. Embrace Challenges as Opportunities

Challenges are a natural part of life, and they are often the key to unlocking new levels of growth. When you embrace difficulties as opportunities rather than obstacles, you cultivate resilience and strength. A limitless mindset sees every challenge as a stepping stone, a lesson to be learned, and a chance to rise higher.

Action Steps:

- **Reframe negative situations**: When faced with a challenge, ask yourself, "What can I learn from this?" Instead of feeling defeated, focus on how the experience can help you grow and improve.

- **Celebrate your perseverance**: Reflect on past challenges you've overcome. Remind yourself how far you've come and how much stronger you've become through adversity.

4. Surround Yourself with Positive Influence

The people you surround yourself with play a crucial role in nurturing your limitless mindset. Positive, uplifting individuals who encourage you to push past your limits and believe in your potential will help you stay on track. Seek out communities, mentors, and friends who share your values and who will challenge you to continue evolving.

Action Steps:

- **Seek out supportive communities**: Whether it's an online group, a mastermind, or a local community, find people who share your ambition and support your vision.

- **Limit exposure to negativity**: Be mindful of who and what you allow to influence your mind. If certain relationships or environments bring you down, create healthy boundaries to protect your mindset.

5. Practice Self-Compassion

Nurturing a limitless mindset is not about being perfect or always succeeding. It's about understanding that growth is a journey and that you are worthy of love and respect throughout it. Self-compassion allows you to bounce back from mistakes, forgive yourself when things don't go as planned, and continue forward with renewed determination.

Action Steps:

- **Be gentle with yourself**: When you make a mistake, instead of beating yourself up, treat yourself with kindness. Remind yourself that failure is part of the learning process.

- **Practice positive self-talk**: Speak to yourself with the same encouragement and support you would offer to a friend. Replace self-criticism with affirmations of strength, resilience, and potential.

6. Celebrate Your Progress

A key to nurturing your limitless mindset is celebrating how far you've come, not just how far you have to go. Acknowledge your achievements, no matter how small, and take time to honor your growth. Celebrating progress fuels your motivation and reinforces the belief that you are capable of achieving more.

Action Steps:

- **Create milestones**: Break your bigger goals into smaller, achievable steps, and celebrate when you reach them. Each milestone serves as a reminder that you are capable of turning your dreams into reality.

- **Reflect on your growth**: Regularly take time to look back at your journey. Reflect on the challenges you've overcome, the lessons you've learned, and how much you've grown. This practice helps you maintain perspective and keep moving forward with confidence.

7. Stay Curious and Open-Minded

A limitless mindset thrives on curiosity—the willingness to ask questions, seek new experiences, and explore new possibilities. Being open-minded allows you to remain flexible, adaptable, and ready to embrace whatever comes your way. It encourages creative thinking, new ideas, and solutions that you might not have considered before.

Action Steps:

- **Try new things**: Push yourself to explore areas outside your comfort zone. Whether it's picking up a new hobby, traveling somewhere unfamiliar, or learning a new skill, novelty keeps your mind open and engaged.

- **Be open to feedback**: Embrace constructive criticism as an opportunity to learn. Don't take it personally, but use it as a stepping stone to bettering yourself.

Conclusion:

Nurturing your limitless mindset is a lifelong process. It requires daily commitment, self-compassion, and a willingness to continue learning and growing. By staying open to life's possibilities, embracing challenges, and surrounding yourself with positivity, you continue to evolve into the person you were always meant to be. The more you cultivate your limitless mindset, the more you'll see the abundance and opportunities that exist in every area of your life.

So, keep nurturing it, keep growing, and never stop believing that you are capable of achieving greatness. Your limitless future is in your hands.

Final Practical Step: Committing to Your New Life

The journey to living a limitless life begins with a single, powerful decision: the commitment to transform your reality. After embracing new perspectives, rewiring your brain, overcoming fears, and nurturing a mindset of abundance, the final step is about making a firm, unwavering commitment to the life you've envisioned and reaffirming the beliefs that will support it. This is the moment you make your new life real—because transformation doesn't just happen in the mind; it's solidified by the actions you take and the promises you make to yourself.

Commitment: The Key to Lasting Change

True transformation requires more than intention; it demands commitment. Committing to your new life means you are no longer a passive observer of your circumstances. You become the active creator of your future, taking full responsibility for your thoughts, actions, and decisions. It's about deciding that you are worthy of the life you desire and that nothing will stand in your way.

Action Steps:

- **Declare your commitment**: Say it out loud or write it down. Make a personal declaration that you are committed to living a limitless life. This could be as simple as, "I am committed to living boldly, confidently, and without limitations."

- **Take consistent action**: Show up for your transformation every single day. Even when things get tough or life feels uncertain, stay committed to your goals. It's the daily choices that ultimately shape your future.

Reaffirming Your Beliefs: The Foundation of Your New Reality

The beliefs you hold shape everything in your life. If you truly want to live a limitless life, it's vital to reaffirm the empowering beliefs that have supported your transformation. These beliefs serve as the foundation upon which your new reality is built. Each time you reaffirm them, you are not only reinforcing your mindset, but you're also reprogramming your subconscious mind to support your journey.

Action Steps:

- **Create a list of empowering beliefs**: Write down a list of beliefs that reflect the person you are becoming. These might include, "I am capable of achieving anything I set my mind to," "I trust that I am always supported by the universe," or "I am worthy of love, success, and abundance." Repeat these affirmations daily.

- **Affirm your beliefs with passion**: When you say your affirmations, do so with energy, conviction, and emotion. Let your words become a powerful mantra that reinforces your limitless potential.

- **Visualize your new life**: Take a few moments every day to visualize your new reality. See yourself already living the life you desire—happy, confident, fulfilled, and aligned with your purpose. This visualization will not only reaffirm your beliefs, but it will also ignite the motivation to take inspired action.

Aligning Your Daily Actions with Your Beliefs

Commitment is not just a one-time decision—it's a daily practice. Aligning your actions with your reaffirmed beliefs means that every choice you make, every step you take, reflects the life you want to create. When your thoughts, words, and actions are in harmony with your vision, you become unstoppable.

Action Steps:

- **Make decisions based on your new beliefs**: When faced with choices, ask yourself, "Does this decision align with the person I am becoming?" Choose the path that reflects your new limitless identity.

- **Create daily rituals**: Build routines that reinforce your new mindset. Whether it's morning affirmations, journaling, or practicing gratitude, these rituals will solidify your commitment and keep you on track.

- **Celebrate each victory**: Every small success along the way is a reflection of your commitment and growth. Celebrate them, no matter how small they may seem. Recognizing your progress keeps you motivated and reinforces your belief in the process.

Embracing the Journey Ahead

The final step in your transformation is to fully embrace the journey. Your limitless life is not an end goal, but a continual unfolding. With every day that passes, you have the opportunity to evolve, grow, and step more fully into the person you are meant to be. Commit to showing up for yourself, to reaffirming your belief in your potential, and to taking the inspired actions that will guide you toward the life you desire.

This is your moment to create lasting change and to live with unwavering confidence, purpose, and joy. Trust in the process, believe in yourself, and keep moving forward. The limitless life you've always dreamed of is within your reach, and the most important part of the journey is already underway—your commitment and belief in your boundless potential.

www.ingramcontent.com/pod-product-compliance
Lightning Source LLC
Chambersburg PA
CBHW021137130626
46554CB00005B/1547